CREATIVE DESTRUCTION
AND THE ELECTRIC UTILITY OF THE FUTURE

Creative Destruction and the Electric Utility of the Future

David J. Hurlbut, Ph.D.

Three Trusts

2017

Copyright © 2017 by David J. Hurlbut

Edited by Annie Hartnett, Artemis Ink. LLC
Cover by Alfred Hicks
Publishing consultant: Rick Lite
Typography by David J. Hurlbut

ISBN   978-0-692-96679-2 (electronic)
        978-0-692-96738-6 (print)

Hurlbut, David J.
Creative Destruction and the Electric Utility of the Future / David J. Hurlbut

Includes bibliographic references and index

Subjects
        Law: public utilities
        Political science: public policy — energy policy
Related themes
        Alternative & renewable energy sources & technology — Climate change — Economic history — Economic theory & philosophy — Energy & power generation & distribution — Energy industries & utilities — Environmental economics — Fossil fuel technologies — Political economy

Printed in the United States of America
First printing

Published by
Three Trusts, Inc.
Golden, Colorado

Visit the web site, http://www.utilitycreativedestruction.com

Dedicated to my parents, Joseph and Lena

Contents

The pride of the cup is in the drink, its humility in the serving. What, then, do its defects matter?

Dag Hammarskjöld

Preface

This book is the result of being in the right place at the right time, several times. My professional and academic experience has left me with a collection of insights into many aspects of a complex component of our economy, and I feel a duty to synthesize these experiences in a way that can make them useful to others. Truth often resides not just with the facts themselves, but in the way facts weave together to form a coherent story. The more complex and mysterious the relationships become, the greater the need to step back and look at the big picture. I believe the evolution of electricity is one such story.

The ideas here are meant to serve as a platform to guide further and more detailed study. If the theory is robust, it will help form relevant research questions that will lead to greater empirical understanding of the challenges the future electricity sector will face. These challenges include (among other things) finding new market design principles that harmonize capital formation with operational efficiency, while at the same time minimizing harmful collateral effects outside the electricity supply chain. They include finding new principles for rate design that enable end-user customers to supply the grid with energy and reliability services. My hope is that this book can serve as a guide for decision makers who are struggling to understand what laws and policies might best respond to new demands on the electricity sector.

The challenges demand that we think outside the box rather than rely on methods grounded in old world thinking. Just as the development of nuclear weapons demanded that scientists start looking at the world differently, the electricity sector's shifting socioeconomic undercurrents are rendering conventional thinking insufficient. As Albert Einstein observed to his fellow scientists at the dawn of the nuclear age:

Our situation is not comparable to anything in the past. It is impossible, therefore, to apply methods and measures which at an earlier age might have been sufficient. We must revolutionize our thinking....[1]

My belief is that if analysis is to address the future power sector in any useful way, it needs to re-ground itself. Without a new paradigm, analysis will remain rooted in the old. A thoughtful public conversation about rethinking the power sector needs to include diverse experts in disciplines that usually have a difficult time talking to one another. This book is a call to invent new synergistic approaches to understand the challenges facing electric utilities.

Several people have aided me in my effort to make holistic sense of what has been happening. I am especially grateful to Pat Wood III for his outstanding leadership as chairman of the Texas Public Utilities Commission (PUC). I had the good professional fortune to be present at the creation of electric sector restructuring in Texas, first as a member of the commissioners' advisory staff and then as a senior economist with the commission's market oversight division. That experience has shaped much of the thinking laid out in this book. Pat's keen intellect kept the very complicated task of restructuring true to its theoretical foundations, but what truly brought it all to a point of success in the real world was his extraordinary ability to listen. New opportunities came with new responsibilities and new risks, and some stakeholders were understandably nervous about what the new world would bring. What some saw as problems, Pat saw as puzzles that reasonable people could figure out with time, dialogue, the right focus, and encouragement for creative thinking.

This work necessarily delves into how the public and private sectors interact with one another. My thinking in this area has been influenced significantly by the late Hon. Barbara Jordan,

---

[1] "Einstein Reveals Text of Message," *New York Times*, August 29, 1948. (Published later under the title "Message to Intellectuals.")

who was one of my professors at University of Texas at Austin's Lyndon B. Johnson School of Public Affairs. In her seminar on public sector ethics, she constantly confronted students with real-world public interest dilemmas and never let anyone get by with easy answers that skipped over important pieces of the problem. But she also taught that these are the problems most in need of solutions, and that one should never give up just because finding answers is hard.

These and many other professional and academic experiences have come together at the National Renewable Energy Laboratory (NREL), where for the past decade I've had the honor of working with an extraordinary group of talented thinkers. The laboratory's leadership, all the way from my colleagues and managers up to former Director Dan Arvizu and current Director Martin Keller, provided a tremendous amount of encouragement in writing this book. They recognized that even though such theoretical work is outside the comfort zone of most entities that fund energy research, it is nevertheless an important emerging theme in sustainable energy.

I am also grateful to my editor, Annie Hartnett, and to my colleagues who read and commented on this book at various stages of its preparation.

Finally, I am immensely grateful to the Rev. Ruth Rinehart— my wife, life partner, and soul mate. Besides giving her love and encouragement, she has helped me think through important ideas and how they are presented in this book. Ruth has kept me mindful of the fact that this book is not just for other energy nerds like me. What is happening can and should be understood by a wider audience.

While I have drawn extensively on my experience from the Texas PUC and NREL to write this book, its observations and conclusions do not represent—and are not intended to represent—the views of anyone besides myself. Indeed, the ability of both these institutions to work as effectively as they do comes in part from the richness of diverse perspectives. Some with whom I have worked no doubt read the same tea leaves differently, and that is fine. I am responsible only for my own reading, not anyone else's.

Chapter 1: Why This Book?

The business of generating and delivering electricity is on the threshold of evolutionary change. The underlying causes are so pervasive, so inexorable, and so removed from convention that current ways of understanding how the power sector works are of limited help in seeing what the future has in store. More customers want to be smart about how they use electricity, they are finding more ways to do it, and their preferences are diverse. The once passive and predictable business relationship between the customer and the electric utility is becoming dynamic, auguring fundamental change in what utilities must do in order to survive.

This book provides a conceptual framework for understanding how the power sector is changing. My goal is to provide a context for the many conversations currently taking place about the so-called "utility of the future." Much of the discussion that has taken place so far has been among specialists who already live and breathe electricity sector issues in great detail. The discussion needs to expand to include people who might find the technical esoterica rather mind-numbing but who will, nevertheless, feel the effects of the socioeconomic metamorphosis taking place. Political decision makers especially need to understand what is happening, why it is happening, and how it is happening. The changes taking place in the electricity sector are intertwined with other public policy issues in complex ways that, more often than not, are beyond a specialist's ability to explain. Unfortunately, this also means that opportunities for strategic disinformation in the political arena will be many. However, a core group of progressive leaders with a well-grounded understanding of the big picture might be in a position to protect the public interest.

Members of the public are also likely to have a growing interest in how their electricity choices are changing, and what it might mean for their lifestyles. The electricity customer is the bedrock economic actor at center stage in this transformation. As explained throughout this book, the utility of the future will provide customers with increasingly diverse choices in electricity service.

It is tempting to think that the utility of the future is all about technological innovation—tempting, but incorrect. Nifty widgets do not cause social evolution. Major socioeconomic shifts come about only when technology intersects with human needs and preferences in a way that liberates widespread aspirations that were previously suppressed, hidden, or unformed. Even then, the role played by "technology" is properly grasped only by taking an expansive approach.

The Greek *tekhnología*, from which the modern word *technology* derives, can be translated as "systematic treatment." This describes how I approach technology in this book. It goes far beyond clever gadgets, encompassing the reshaping of institutional arrangements, new patterns of social decision making, and the revised logic of economic rationality. For the electric utility of the future, disruptive technology is a very rarified subset of inventions that must be judged by how they affect economic choices in the real world. If a new technology is disruptive (and few truly are), it is because it engenders a compelling market demand that does not fit into the existing modes of systematic treatment—*tekhnología*—commonly used to make socioeconomic decisions. A new gadget that engenders no substantial new demand is little more than a pebble bouncing off the machine of convention, passing away unnoticed.

Historically, the clash between old and new has caused several stress points in how utilities operate and how regulators oversee them. In some cases, the pace of technological change is forcing decision makers into unfamiliar areas where precedent is absent and institutions are ill-equipped. The problem is that legislation and docketed proceedings normally address one problem at a time. Addressing the new challenges in this old manner could draw society into a protracted game of regulatory whack-a-mole, where fixing the issue-du-jour could have unintended consequences that only lead to new problems popping up tomorrow.

We've been here before. Rotary telephones are today a fading memory, in much the same way that horse-drawn carriages all but disappeared during the years after Henry Ford began mass producing the Model T. Society is once again facing a time of creative destruction, where the opportunities afforded by new inventions are forcing old processes and customs into obsolescence.

Such fundamental shifts do not happen overnight. Like a changing global climate, the metamorphosis is gradual and sometimes not apparent in what we see and can measure in the moment. Certainly, there are, as of this writing, many large coal-fired generating stations still in operation, and it is unlikely that every one of them will be permanently shut down before this decade is out. But the coal fleet's existence today does nothing to disprove the broad-based and long-term economic shifts taking place—just like standing on a porch during one sub-zero day in North Dakota does not disprove the evidence that global temperatures are rising generally. Nor does the existence of operating coal plants today negate the fact that these shifts are converging to create a new economic environment in which building more coal plants will be financially impossible.

The discussion in the chapters that follow is theoretical. Its purpose is to synthesize a wide array of observable facts into a story that is both coherent and useful. The reader will find no complex equations, no advanced quantitative models, no exhaustive case studies, no "analysis" as that term is commonly applied. All of that comes later. If the world truly is changing (as evidence suggests), analysis based on old world theories will always circle around to old world conclusions. My goal here is to develop a new theory that poses new testable hypotheses, so that future analysis will be more aligned with where the electricity sector is actually headed.

On-the-ground reality will be different from one market to the next, and that is to be expected. Circumstantial differences do not invalidate a theory. Rather, if it is a sound theory, it will necessarily play out differently in different situations. Thus, the utility of the future will not look the same everywhere, nor will any two paths to it be identical.

The signs of imminent change are upon us, more visible in some places than in others. It is difficult to say when all the forces will reach a critical mass in any given market. Most likely, it will happen at different times in different places. Politics will be a key variable affecting the pace: To what extent will entrenched interests succeed in getting elected leaders to interfere with the economic forces leading the industry into a new paradigm?

This book and its theoretical foundations are rooted in experiences in the United States—admittedly a shortcoming for more global applications, but prudent for the primary audience I hope to reach. Conceptualizing the utility of the future in a U.S. context allows me as an author to draw on my own experience and to delve more deeply into the nuances of the transition taking place. It also permits better consideration of the historical and cultural factors that color the change as it plays out in the United States. I do this fully recognizing that issues might (and most likely will) play out differently in the economies of other countries. I leave those analyses to others who are at home in these different cultural circumstances.

I begin the book by discussing two foundational matters—the public interest and economics. I use these perspectives to focus on technological changes in the wholesale supply chain and on end-use customer behavior. They reveal that the tension between monopoly and competition is growing throughout the wholesale supply chain. Born of technological advances, these tensions have economic and public policy ramifications that cannot be addressed without fundamentally rethinking what it means to be a utility. Similarly, the field of retail customer possibilities and preferences is diversifying, creating its own set of economic and public policy tensions.

The last two chapters focus on how these theoretical threads weave together. They explore what the utility of the future might look like, and what this new world might demand of those in government whose job it will be to regulate it.

First Lens: The Public Interest

Asking what the utility of the future will look like begins with questioning what it means to be a utility in the first place, and that begins with an inquiry into the public interest.

Common law has long recognized that a business enterprise can be "clothed with a public interest" if it occupies a pivotal and irreplaceable position in the economy. A heightened level of regulatory oversight over these special enterprises was considered justified, because the damage wrought by failure, incompetence, or chicanery would ripple throughout the economy.

Electric utility regulation has been around almost as long as electric utilities themselves. Early on, the public interest in regulating electricity service had to do with public easements, and then later antitrust and the need to restrain the power of monopolies. These goals shaped many important aspects of what I call the "regulatory contract" between the State and the utility: the bundle of economic freedoms surrendered by the enterprise and the economic protections underwritten by the State. Many of the institutional practices that arose from this original regulatory contract continue today.

In recent decades, however, technological advances have fragmented what used to be a vertically integrated utility enterprise, and a growing number of these activities are no longer natural monopolies. Competition and the right of customers to choose are emerging as new elements of the public interest.

The production and delivery of electricity, moreover, are now recognized to be intertwined with other social imperatives. We know more than we did half a century ago about the world and how it works as a network of networks, weaving numerous anthropological systems together with systems of the natural environment. This has ethical ramifications for how utility decisions are made because it recognizes that the generation of electricity has effects far beyond the traditional concerns about cost and reliability.

Technological change, the erosion of monopoly, and a more diverse array of consumer preferences have made it necessary to step back and revisit what it means to be an electric utility and which aspects of such a utility truly need to be regulated. In short: the public interest is changing, and these changes are guiding what the next generation of utilities will look like and how they will work.

Second Lens: The Economics of Creative Destruction

At the heart of the disruptive changes are economic forces that are rewriting the rules for the formation and use of capital in the production of electricity. Under the old regulatory contract, the public interest shaped regulatory practices for capital investment on the assumption that electric utilities were a natural monopoly. This included special protections from risk that enhanced capital formation, giving utilities advantages not enjoyed by other industrial sectors when it came to attracting investment. The erosion of natural monopoly reduces the need for these protections, and this changes the very nature of capital formation.

Austrian economist Joseph Schumpeter was one of the first to think in larger social terms about how entrepreneurship and technological advances can combine to trigger disruptive economic change. Schumpeter wrote about how firms compete to be the first to secure new processes and inventions, thereby gaining a technological edge over rivals. With this tendency replicated across all businesses, capitalism creates, devours, and discards one *tekhnología* after another. Schumpeter's observations aptly describe what has happened to telecommunications and information technology more recently. Once again, economic undercurrents seem to be converging towards a perfect "Schumpeterian storm," this time in the electric sector.

The *tekhnología* enabling this storm combines new information systems with new institutional approaches to social decision-making. As monopoly ceases to be the natural order of things in the electricity sector, competition strives to step in wherever it can. Prudent capital investment in a competitive market demands more astute risk management, something that weighed less heavily on old-world utilities. The regulatory contract provided utilities with a reasonably bankable guarantee that infrastructure investments—approved by the State—would always be backed by rate revenue collected from the utility's captured customer base. In the utility of the future by contrast, non-utility merchant generators have no comparable institutional backstop and are on the hook themselves for any errors in judgment. This disciplines how they compare options for attracting and applying capital. At the same time, it places a burden on market prices to be right. Prices need to respond accurately to supply and demand, and they must be immune from abuses of market power or other distortions.

The central characters in this economic drama are *gigaplants*: large central station thermal generating plants whose capacity is measured in gigawatts. The privileged economic conditions that enabled an extraordinary period of gigaplant expansion in the 1970s and 1980s began unraveling in the early 2000s, and these conditions will never return. Tectonic shifts in the economic environment have set gigaplants on the road to extinction.

The economic change that has begun to play out constitutes a true sea change, not something that is happening simply because of federal or state policy decisions. If anything, "progressive" policy is following the change and adapting to it, not causing it. Nor is there any turning back. Like standing in the middle of a raging river and trying to push back against it, political attempts to stop the course of economic evolution are ultimately futile and risk inflicting considerable harm on society.

Focus on Fragmentation

States that have restructured their electric sectors to allow competition have demonstrated that under the right conditions power generation, delivery, and retail customer service can be unbundled into separate business enterprises. Unbundling is a key step in the dissolution of natural monopoly and the emergence of competition.

Competition is a creature with many appetites. It can create efficiency and add to the good of society, while other aspects can be pathological and economically disruptive. The markets that arise with fragmentation, therefore, require careful design and vigilant monitoring. If market outcomes are to replace regulatory judgment, the market environment needs to be fair and transparent.

The public-interest value of competition is greater economic efficiency to the benefit of society as a whole. For this to occur, price signals throughout the market must be meaningful. Price signals are the nerve impulses by which the many independent parts of the market body function together in a healthy, efficient whole. When working as they should, prices attract response when there are opportunities for greater efficiency, and deter behaviors that tend to impose needless costs on the system.

Fragmenting monopoly makes the economics of daily operations and capital investment less forgiving of mistakes and sloppy planning. Errors—even those made in good faith after prudent risk assessment—carry economic consequences for the power generator and its investors. Unlike old-world utilities, there is no financial backstop underwritten by the public.

Some parts of the United States have already unbundled their utilities. As well, areas served by regional transmission organizations operate as fragmented wholesale markets where energy dispatch and reliability are managed through competitive mechanisms. Each of these areas had a learning curve during which market rules evolved and market participants became accustomed to the new paradigm. Getting market design right takes time, and is an on-going process.

Focus on Customer Liberation

The hallmark of the future electric utility will be the liberation of consumer preferences. No longer will all customers need to be treated the same. Consumer preferences are becoming more sophisticated and diverse, leading to a metamorphosis in the retail electricity market that parallels the dissolution of the natural monopoly in electricity production.

Not all customers will exercise the choice available to them, but that itself is part of consumer diversification. In the electric utility of the future any customer will be able to choose to not choose and continue to enjoy the convenience of generic service. What is less defensible, however, is to force all customers into the straightjacket of standardization just because some prefer convenience. There is no longer any need to do so.

Linked with greater choice for customers is the more sophisticated use of price signals by the utility. In the future, *all* retail rates will incentivize behaviors that reduce system costs and penalize those that add to costs. As a result, the convenience of not choosing will come with a price premium in the form of potential savings that the customer decides to forego.

Low-cost information technology and entrepreneurial innovation will enable electricity customers to be dynamic market participants—not just passive consumers of a commodity. The customer potentially can wear two hats: that of a consumer, as well as that of a producer. Up to now, customer-sited generation such as rooftop solar has largely been treated as an adjustment to the customer's usage, with the customer's final bill based on the net difference between what was consumed and what was produced on the customer's side of the meter. In the future utility, the aggregation of customer-sited generation will be managed, monitored, and paid separately from consumption, similar to large-scale generators. This system will also make use of price signals, so that small-scale generators capable of providing extra value to the grid will be paid more.

The oil crises of the 1970s demonstrate how the maturation of customer demand affects the ability to respond to price signals. At that time, commercial and industrial customers had both the experience and the means (through their rate structures) to respond to the economically brutal energy price signals resulting from the 1973 Arab Oil Embargo and the oil supply shock of 1979-80. Residential customers, by contrast, did not. Individuals were just moving into a new phase where electricity was becoming integral to household lifestyles, and the rates used by utilities were too simplistic to provide much of a price signal. Using less electricity would have meant doing without essentials such as heating, air conditioning, and refrigeration. So, while the oil crises brought about a clear shift towards energy efficiency for commercial and industrial customers, data for the residential sector suggests no similar movement towards efficiency until the Great Recession of 2008 and 2009.

Today residential and nonresidential customers alike are more sophisticated. They have more choices in how they use electricity, although in many areas residential customers are still held back by antiquated rate structures that are not capable of translating cost-reducing behaviors into customer value. Despite utilities' piecemeal efforts at adaptation, liberated customers do not fit within a utility's traditional business model. The changes taking place require that utilities rise to the challenge of meeting the needs of more sophisticated and liberated customers.

The Market Maker

Neither wholesale market fragmentation nor customer choice is a self-driving car, regardless of how strong the economic forces behind them might be. Markets can be manipulated. Customers can be deceived. For the electric sector's post-monopoly economic order to truly move the public good forward, the markets on which they are based must operate fairly and efficiently. This gives rise to a new role in the future utility: the *market maker*.

In organized wholesale markets, regional transmission organizations perform the market maker function. They run the information systems used to dispatch generators on the network on a least-cost basis. These organizations have no direct interest in any generator or load-serving entity. Significantly, this new wholesale function for managing competition among merchant generators is itself a natural monopoly.

At the retail level, the market maker will be the distribution utility that manages the physical flow of electricity to end-use customers. It will meter the energy that customers use, and will manage the flow of usage-related data for the many electricity service providers competing for retail customers. The data managed by the market maker will enable competitive retail providers to bill their subscribing customers correctly, and it will let customers verify that the service they received was what they paid for.

The operational knowledge used by the market maker will comprise the traditional utility's control center, distribution operations, and transmission operations. These functions can be spun off into independent regulated companies, or they can be organizationally segregated from the rest of the utility's operations and treated as a distinct regulated subsidiary. Whatever its form, the market maker's operations would continue to be overseen by the State because it would be a natural monopoly. One new aim of regulation will be to socialize the fair cost of market making functions and to keep the market maker at a healthy arm's length from the financial outcomes of the companies competing in the wholesale and retail markets.

Updating the Regulatory Contract

The public interest, capital formation, competition, and customer aspirations are propelling the electricity sector to an entirely new way of being. But can regulators—whose fundamental charge is safeguarding the public interest—keep up? The price signals on which many elements of this new world will depend require well-designed electricity rate structures. However, ratemaking is bound up with regulatory conventions that are colliding with the electric sector's transformation. Some adaptation has already occurred as a result of restructuring, but there are indications that the process of creative destruction is outpacing regulatory reform in some places.

The regulators' role as rate setters and approvers of investment is diminishing. The utility of the future is creating the need for a new regulatory role that may be described as the "market cop" walking the economic beat. This new type of regulator will have a close relationship with the utility performing the role of market maker. It will delineate the authority and procedures by which the market maker can set and revise protocols for daily operations. When there is disagreement about the intrinsic fairness of a market outcome, the regulator will be the one that adjudicates the complaint.

Being essentially a regulated utility, the market maker will never have the legal standing to prosecute civil or criminal charges when a competitor deliberately causes mischief in the market. That burden will necessarily remain with the State. The market maker will act instead as the expert witness, providing advice and access to evidence residing in its market data systems. But the final determination of guilt, the weighing of extenuating circumstances, and the assessment of penalty will be part of the State's police power, exercised through the regulator, the State's prosecutors, and the courts.

The regulator will also need to do what neither the market maker nor individual market participants will be positioned to do: consider the market from a long-term, high-level perspective. Market processes are necessarily short-term. When functioning well they can achieve outcomes that are optimal *based on current conditions*. A local, short-term optimum is not necessarily the same as a global, long-term optimum, however. A crucial role for the regulator in the new utility paradigm will be to monitor long-term market outcomes to determine whether the design of the market consistently leads to sub-optimal results.

The State's role, therefore, will not go away. As matters like price determination move from regulatory proceedings to the market, the role of the regulator will shift from price-setting to fostering competition in the market. Achieving the public interest in this new utility model will depend on competition that is fair, open, and nondiscriminatory.

The Electric Utility of the Future

All of this brings us to the electric utility of the future.

For many customers, electricity service will be something they shop for online, just like they shop for many other goods and services today. Unlike their old electric service, the utility of the future will offer choices: discounted rates for use at night or on the weekend, all renewable, variable price, fixed price, and many other options that will make it possible to build a customized service package suited to individual preferences. Customers will be able to compare prices, look at complaint and satisfaction ratings, and check product claims. They will be able to decide for themselves how to balance low cost with low environmental impact.

The providers offering these choices will be many. They will be the electricity "buyers clubs" that aggregate retail customers with similar preferences. Each of these buyers clubs will connect with the distribution utility acting as the area's retail market maker. The utility will ensure that each retail buyers club gets the detailed consumption data needed to accurately bill customers, and each buyers club will provide the market maker with daily forecasts of how its customers will use electricity so that the utility can ensure reliability.

A buyers club will also negotiate supply deals directly with companies that generate electricity. Because each buyers club will be competing for its own customers, each will use its mass buying power to negotiate power purchase agreements at prices and terms most favorable to its customers.

As *tekhnología* evolves, third-party entrepreneurs will find profitable ways to help a broader range of customers save money. The savviest customers will want to take advantage of "smart" electricity meters, smart appliances, and home energy management systems that can adapt consumption patterns to price signals in the customer's service plan.

This liberation of choice will also mean that a customer's bill at the end of the month will carry the consequences of cost-saving and cost-causing behaviors. Efficient customers will no longer be subsidizing inefficient ones.

On the production side, the demand for operational efficiency will be intense. Without a publicly underwritten backstop to cover mistakes, inefficiency, and poor investments, companies in the business of generating electricity will need to be more astute in reducing their costs to a point that balances profits and competitiveness. They will be forced to manage the risks.

The economics of the new market will value production flexibility. Natural gas generators provide operational flexibility but are vulnerable to volatile fuel prices. To hedge against the inevitable ups and downs of natural gas prices, a well-rounded portfolio will also include renewables, which are heavy on stable long-term capital costs but carry no volatile fuel costs.

The wholesale market maker will open up electricity production to smaller and more diverse resources. This will include end-use customers themselves—those who have their own on-site generation resources, as well as those who have the flexibility to reduce their electricity use on a moment's notice if the price is right. Information systems operated by the market maker and populated with data from groups of retail customers aggregated and managed by a buyers club will, as the processes improve, make thousands of small-scale resources perform like a larger plant.

One big thing will *not* be in the picture: new gigaplants. The utility of the future will lack the regulatory assurances that were essential to these leviathans' capital formation. Thus, as these aging coal and nuclear giants reach the end of their economic lives, they will die without offspring—not because of any government policy but because their capital-forming DNA will no longer fit in the new economic environment.

The growing pains will extend further, however. Some policies that have been important to early adoption of renewables and other clean energy technologies won't fit well in the new paradigm. While losing these tools may seem to undermine clean energy deployment, the real effect is rather different. The path to maximum adoption of clean energy technologies in both the near and distant future necessarily passes through an evolutionary landscape. Clinging to old-world tools such as net metering will only result in slower and less efficient adoption over the long term. The new world will work differently and will need new approaches.

The utility of the future is not about technology; it's about choice and competition. It's not about the role of government going away; it's about government taking on a new role. Government is not causing or orchestrating it, but it can smooth the way.

Chapter 2: The Public Interest

Of all the forces of change that are pushing utilities into an uncharted future, the public interest is perhaps the most difficult to measure. The public interest as a general concept might seem easy to grasp at first, but it gets more complicated as more individuals and more diverse interests enter the picture. The public interest is not simply the least common denominator across an array of private interests; it is an affirmative expression of social values. When private interests eventually come into irreconcilable conflict, society decides who wins and who loses based on its articulation of the public interest.

Technology and rational analysis inform such decisions, but they cannot by themselves resolve what the public interest is. Engineers, scientists, economists, and other analysts often treat public interest questions as being out of their scope and avoid addressing them. Nevertheless, the public interest often determines whether a technical study has enough social relevance to make a meaningful contribution to the public good. As a result, the public interest will continue to be an important factor—if not the most important factor—in determining what the utility of the future will look like and how it will evolve. Technology can enable options, and analysis can help separate fact from fiction. Ultimately, however, decisions taken in the public interest will rest on more.

Throughout most of the 20th Century, the public interest with respect to the provision of electricity was uncomplicated. For convenience, I summarize it as follows:

It is in the public interest for society to enjoy the benefits of electric power at the least cost with the greatest reliability.

Cost has been of primary significance to the public interest. Every rate case that comes before a state utility commission, city council, or electric cooperative's governing board is scrutinized and challenged by consumer advocates whose primary objective is to keep costs as low as possible. A new capital investment could very well be on the cutting edge of technological advancement, but the utility must still demonstrate how the investment will leave customers better off. If the case isn't made, the investment remains little more than a shiny toy for the utility's engineers. Only if the utility succeeds in proving need for the investment, does the public interest allow for the utility to recover that cost from customers through its rates.

Reliability has also been an essential part of the public interest. Lights should come on when you flip the switch. Voltage should not spike to the point of causing damage to electric motors and other devices. Past a certain point, however, each incremental improvement in reliability becomes more difficult and costly to achieve. The rule of diminishing returns applies to system reliability. Perfect reliability can be economically impractical if not technically impossible.

The need to balance cost and reliability has not gone away, but new elements of public good have entered into the mix. The many spheres of the natural world and of human activity are overlapping with greater complexity, intensity, and visibility. As a result, the public interest with respect to electricity is no longer easily separated from other public interest concerns such as environmental protection and social justice. At the end of this chapter I will propose a restatement of the public interest that accounts for these concerns.

The changing public interest affects many kinds of decisions about regulating the production and delivery of electricity. The allocation of cost, for example, has deep public interest ramifications. New technology might be innovative and helpful, but it is never free. Reaching a defensible decision on who pays and what share they pay is impossible without a clear vision of the public interest. This is part of the cultural shift being ushered in by the future utility.

Nuances in true costs have largely been swept under the rug of convenience and socialized for most of the electric sector's commercial history.[2] This practice is ethically benign when all customers generally use electricity in the same way, with deviations from the norm (deviations that cause unusual costs) randomly distributed among the customer base. Once usage begins to diverge into several distinct and consistent patterns, differences in cost causation tend to become more systematic, resulting in some customers consistently creating additional costs and other customers systematically paying for costs they did not cause. The decision to socialize some costs and to directly assign others to the customers who caused them is an issue of the public interest.

Another public interest issue is how customer information is shared. Many new technologies are data-intensive, and entities besides the utility could be involved in turning all that information into value for the customer and for society. Finding a balance between privacy, security, and the creation of economic value—all against a backdrop of increasing cybersecurity threats —is crucial to the public interest.

The public interest can mean different things to different people, so I start this chapter with an explanation of what I mean when I use the term. I beg the reader's patience in this. While it might seem tedious, it is essential. There is little point thinking about what the utility of the future will be if one does

---

[2] By "socialized," I mean that within a given class of customer (residential, commercial, or industrial) all of the costs allocated to that class are assessed to all members using mostly the same pro rata metric such as cents per kilowatt-hour. Residential customers are commonly charged largely by the kilowatt-hours they use, without distinguishing between times when the cost of generation is high and when it is low. This is beginning to change in some markets with the deployment of advanced meters and the development of time-of-use rate plans.

not start with a clear understanding of what it means to be a utility in the first place. That, as this chapter will explain, requires an understanding of the public interests that are at play. Too often, technical analyses of how the electricity sector is changing (or should change) skip such questions by falling back on worn-out bromides about the inability of political, legal, and social institutions to keep up with technological change. In my view, that dismissiveness is part of what needs to change.

What follows is my own view of the public interest, which others can agree with or not. Ultimately, the public interest is distilled through public discourse and actualized through public institutions. This is my contribution to the discussion as it pertains to the creation and delivery of electricity. I begin with some foundational matters involving social values and notions of human nature that have long contended for dominance in the public interest arena. These ethical yardsticks test the potential implications of technological change against the social institutions that would act on them.

Public Interest Theory and the Regulatory Contract

The relationship between the utility and the State can be characterized as a *regulatory contract*.[3] The utility surrenders to the State certain key business decisions, such as pricing. In exchange the State grants certain protections, such as a guaranteed rate of return and the right to operate without competition. The regulatory contract derives from what social scientists and philosophers often refer to as the *social contract*, although it is more narrowly focused. The regulatory contract manifests in laws and regulations that govern the utility. These rules arise from the history, norms, and assumptions weaving the public interest fabric from which the rules are cut.

---

[3] I use "State" (capitalized) as a convention referring to government generically, be it national, subnational or local. A city council as well as an electric cooperative's governing board are included under the term State.

The social contract concerns the relationship between the individual and society—particularly the tradeoffs between individual rights and community responsibility. Absolute individual liberty might be workable for a lone survivor marooned on a deserted island, but chaos ensues when the island becomes populated by many individuals each bent on securing his or her own absolute liberty by any means. Only in the context of a community do things like justice and fairness have meaning. Indeed, one thread of human evolution has been the way society determines what justice is: from "might makes right," to the divine right of monarchs and the aristocracy, to—more recently—the rule of law.

On the other hand, absolute social control with no individual liberty is the stuff of dystopian science fiction. In fact, the aspiration of liberty within community lies at the heart of the U.S. Constitution, which proclaims its goal to "secure the Blessings of Liberty to ourselves and our posterity." More recently, civil rights movements have been movements toward liberty for groups that at various times have labored under the yoke of control by the dominant culture.

The social contract strives for a workable middle ground in the complex space between individual liberty and community responsibility. The ideal social contract increases opportunity for each individual and expands the number of individuals who can enjoy those opportunities.

Anyone working in or with the public sector knows that while this sounds good and virtuous, it is far from easy to achieve. When individuals are gathered into a community, the dynamics of personal relationships and individual aspirations become exponentially complex. One group action can have many effects, several of which can be unforeseen and unintended. Consequently, there really is no end state to the social contract. Rather, it is a continual process of trial, error, and incremental improvement. The United States began with the ideal goal of individual liberty enshrined in its Constitution but took nearly a century to rid itself of slavery and codify the value of equal protection under the law for all citizens regardless of race or creed. Even with this evolution in the Constitution, making it so day to day is a continuing struggle.[4]

From Aristotle up to the present day, social contract theory has been the story of struggle between two philosophical strands of thought.[5] One is often described by ethicists and philosophers as *deontological*—put simply, the position that what is socially good must be universally good. Looking at the concept through a theological lens, God (the Latin *Deo*) is in every person, and this constitutes the true nature of being (*ontologia*) for every person. The secular analogue is the value that everyone begins from a position of equality before the laws of society. Every person has inherent worth and dignity, creating an ethical obligation for the State to treat each person with equal respect and their interests with equal weight before the law. The Equal Protection Clause, part of the Fourteenth Amendment to the U.S. Constitution, is decidedly deontological: "...nor shall any State deprive any person of life, liberty, or property, without due process of

---

[4] Perhaps the most timeless statement of this principle was made by U.S. Rep. Barbara Jordan, the first African-American woman elected to Congress from Texas. "[W]e heard the beginning of the Preamble to the Constitution of the United States: 'We, the people.' It's a very eloquent beginning. But when that document was completed on the seventeenth of September in 1787, I was not included in that 'We, the people.' I felt somehow for many years that George Washington and Alexander Hamilton just left me out by mistake. But through the process of amendment, interpretation, and court decision, I have finally been included in 'We, the people.' " Statement on the Articles of Impeachment against President Richard M. Nixon, House Judiciary Committee, July 25, 1974.

[5] I have borrowed the deontological-teleological framework from John Rawls. See *A Theory of Justice* (Cambridge: Harvard University Press, 1971) and *Justice as Fairness: A Restatement* (Cambridge: Harvard University Press, 2001).

law; nor deny to any person within its jurisdiction the equal protection of the laws."

Immanuel Kant's Categorical Imperative is one expression of deontological thought. Kant's test is whether one can "[a]ct only according to that maxim whereby you can at the same time will that it should become a universal law without contradiction." That is, the value of a benefit (or conversely, the value of avoiding a harm) must be compellingly positive regardless of which individual stands as the recipient. Or to put it in a more familiar way: "In everything do to others as you would have them do to you; for this is the law and the prophets."[6]

The other approach, which ethicists often describe as *teleological*, measures social good by its combined effect on all society. Some members of society may lose out, but a public decision still could be ethical if the aggregate welfare increases. This is the major difference between the teleological and deontological frameworks.

Utilitarianism is a common expression of this take on the social contract. Happiness is the conceptual metric for "good" in a utilitarian world. With respect to community and relationships between individuals, actions are morally good if they increase the happiness of society as a whole. Raising the teleological bar a bit higher, some hold that a change from the status quo is acceptable if it leaves most members of society better off and no member of society worse off.

Over time classical economics became the teleological handmaid of the public interest. Its foundational works, which arose concurrently with the transition from mercantilism to early industrialism in the 18th and 19th centuries, reflected a sense of the social good that was clearly additive. John Stuart Mill's "Greatest Happiness Principle," for example, holds actions to be "right in proportion as they tend to promote happiness, wrong as

---

[6] Matthew 7:12, New Revised Standard Version (NRSV) of the Bible.

they tend to produce the reverse of happiness." He then puts utilitarianism's foundational principle in a macroeconomic light:

A sacrifice which does not increase, or tend to increase, the sum total of happiness, it considers as wasted. The only self-renunciation which it applauds, is devotion to the happiness, or to some of the means of happiness, of others; either of mankind collectively, or of individuals within the limits imposed by the collective interests of mankind.[7]

Over time, the ethical premises of utilitarianism abetted economists' precision-envy of physics and other natural sciences. Subsequently, happiness came to be seen as a function of wealth because wealth could be quantified, and quantification opened a world of analytical possibility. The result has been quantitative analytical tools such as cost-benefit analysis, econometrics, and input/output models that formalize the teleological paradigm with numerical rigor.[8]

A Thought Experiment

Many of the philosophical tensions bound up with the social contract affect the more focused space of the regulatory contract addressed in this book. A thought experiment might help illustrate how this happens. Consider the ancient homeland of an indigenous tribe, located in a valley where low-cost hydroelectric

---

[7] John Stuart Mill, *Utilitarianism* (London: Parker, Son, and Bourn, 1863), p. 24.

[8] Of course, this logical sequence holds only if one assumes that non-monetary happiness is irrelevant, or at least does not confound the logic of monetized happiness. Economist Herman Daly and theologian John B. Cobb write that mainstream economics is often guilty of "misplaced concreteness" in its proclivity for reducing socioeconomic activity to wealth and measurable factors of production. They argue instead that economics and the environment are best reconciled through a systems approach that accounts for the organic interdependencies linking human activities and the natural world. Daly and Cobb, *For the Common Good: Redirecting the Economy toward Community, the Environment, and a Sustainable Future* (Boston: Beacon Street Press, 1994).

power is viable. The tribe's culture is such that no member would voluntarily surrender their homeland at any price. But the tribe has no veto power over the mobilization of capital and labor towards building the dam. That decision rests with the State.

A teleological ethos would favor relocating the tribe, building the dam, flooding the valley, and using some of the social benefits of hydropower and irrigation to compensate the tribe for the permanent loss of its homeland. The State might include additional compensation to the tribe in recognition of its non-monetary cultural losses. However, any such compensation would be treated as merely an additional line item addressed in the cost-benefit analysis informing the decision to build the dam. If the societal benefits were large enough, building the dam would ultimately produce the greatest good for the greatest number, and would therefore be in the public interest.

A deontological ethos would reach the opposite conclusion. The suffering that dislocation would inflict on the tribe could not be wholly compensated and (more crucial to the deontological framework) would be just as unacceptable to other individuals or tribes if they were to face a similar situation.[9] Forced economic compensation would be even more problematic ethically if the tribe's culture did not measure well-being entirely in monetary terms, or if it weighed the interests of future generations differently than the dominant culture does.

This is the problem of eminent domain. That is, under what conditions is it in the public interest for the State to seize or force access to private property? Eminent domain has been a deontological-teleological tension in the regulatory contract between the utility and society from the beginning. In the early days, the ability to provide electric lighting to customers willing to pay for it depended on running distribution lines across all property—public and private—between where the company could build its

---

[9] I set aside strategic bargaining for this thought experiment; holding out for a better deal is merely a detour back to the teleological.

generator and where its customers lived. The lines encroached on all citizens within the service area regardless of whether they intended to be lighting customers. Thus, City Hall made the first crude attempts at crafting the regulatory contract for electric service.

When technology leads to changes in the functioning of public institutions such as electric utilities, there are public interest ramifications that could change just as radically as the technology. Eminent domain is but one example. Public interest theory's teleological and deontological strands offer two complementary ways to test some of these ramifications, which I do at several points in this chapter. How technologically induced changes and their effects measure up against these ethical standards will help shed light on the institutional and economic changes that can smooth the road leading to the electric utility of the future.

The Utility as an Instrument for the Public Interest

Understanding what the utility of the future *will be* needs to start with a clear vision of what it means to be a utility at all. The relationship between the State and the utility is different from the way governments interact with other business enterprises. Indeed, a loose and undisciplined understanding of what it means to be a utility is a flaw common to many analyses about the future power sector.

Long before electric utilities came into being, there was a recognition that some economic enterprises were "affected with a public interest" and were thus different from enterprises that were strictly private. But the public interest is a function of conditions in society that can change over time. Consequently, a regulated enterprise's "utility-ness" can also change over time. If the relationship between the State and the enterprise it regulates remains fixed in the face of an evolving public interest, then the relationship could cease to be something that promotes the true public interest and could even begin to harm it.

The notion that a utility is "affected with a public interest" was established as a principle in U.S. jurisprudence by the Supreme Court in 1877. That landmark decision, *Munn v. Illinois*, drew on common law principles dating back to the 16th Century.[10] At issue was whether grain elevators that controlled the gateway of agricultural commerce could be regulated by the State of Illinois. Writing for the court majority, Chief Justice Waite said that it was "apparent that all the elevating facilities through which these vast productions 'of seven or eight great States of the West' must pass on the way 'to four or five of the States on the seashore' may be a 'virtual' monopoly." The court found that being a virtual monopoly clothed the elevators with a public interest, and "when private property is devoted to a public use, it is subject to public regulation."

While *Munn v. Illinois* does not entirely lift the fog about what exactly makes a utility, it does provide a compass. Understanding what it means to be a utility begins with figuring out what public interests are at stake.

Running through early regulation during the Renaissance was an implicit desire for a well-ordered political economy. The right of an individual business owner or tradesman to determine prices, enter into contracts, and engage in commerce generally was foundational. Implicit then, as today, was the idea that the economic arena in which individuals engaged in commerce should be fair. "Fair" does not mean risk-free. Acumen, individual preparation, and luck remain the variables that determine commercial success or failure. It does mean—and did mean in 16th century England—that if a private supplier and a private customer can agree to terms that are mutually acceptable, no intermediary force should be able to place capricious barriers between them.

---

[10]*Munn v. State of Illinois*, 94 U.S. 113; 24 L. Ed. 77 (1877).

In the early legal history of State regulation, the threat was monopoly. Unchecked, such leverage could enable excessive surcharges on all normal commerce, and could limit the creation of alternatives. Concerns about monopoly commonly involved transportation: tolls for road access, wharf charges, and even wages paid to wagoners and other common carriers. These services were held to be essential to a well-ordered economy, which therefore justified heightened scrutiny by the State for reasonableness. Commercial activities that were solely private needed no special public scrutiny because they were numerous enough, diverse enough, and independent enough that no single instance of failure, incompetence, or chicanery could significantly harm the economy.[11] In contrast, the few services that common law held to be clothed with a public interest occupied a pivotal position in the economy at large. Failure, incompetence, or chicanery there had consequences that could ripple through the entire sphere of commerce. This is one measure of the difference between public interest and private interest. Where individual decisions lead to outcomes that affect only the individuals involved, the interests are private. Actions with consequences for society—or at the very least, for individuals who had no part in making the decisions—go beyond private interests.

Nevertheless, common law's broad treatment of monopoly blithely stepped over ambiguities and contradictions that lay slumbering until the Industrial Age and rise of representative democracy. Unanswered in common law was whether monopoly is fundamentally a peculiar market characteristic of supply and demand, or whether it begins as a privilege expressly granted by the State. To put it another way: Should the government regulate an enterprise *because* it has inherent market power, or does

---

[11] Regulation differs from the prosecution of fraud and breach of contract in private cases. Civil or criminal harm occurs after the laws are in place, and case for harm is built on evidence in the context of the private interests involved. Regulation, on the other hand, pre-determines the regulated enterprise's commercial decisions going forward.

the government *bestow* market power on an enterprise through the grant of a regulated franchise?

The latter view—that an enterprise was clothed with the public interest only when the State affirmatively created the franchise—was expressed in a dissent to the majority opinion in *Munn v Illinois*. Justice Field wrote that "it is only where some privilege in the bestowal of the government is enjoyed in connection with the property, that it is affected with a public interest in any proper sense of the terms. It is the public privilege conferred with the use of the property which creates the public interest in it." Justice Field's dissent cites the same sources in common law that Chief Justice Waite cites in the majority opinion, but Field applies this alternative interpretation to the term "public interest." His aim is to argue against what he saw as a government incursion into the Fourteenth Amendment of the U.S. Constitution.[12]

By relying on common law, however, Field draws from a time when the power of the State was anything but circumspect. The crown's pleasure determined what franchises were granted and to whom. With little due process involved, there was no need to set in writing any economic, social, or legal criteria that would bind the crown when deciding whether to grant a franchise. It was enough to assume the king would know a monopoly when he saw it (or chose to create it).

Regulation's reach did not have to be long when the major factors of commerce were land, skills, tradesman tools, and basic infrastructure in the form of roads, bridges, and ports. Entrepreneurial capitalism changed that. Railroads, telegraph, gas service, and eventually the generation of electricity opened up

---

[12] The amendment was ratified and added to the Constitution just nine years before the Supreme Court decided *Munn v. Illinois*. The first section of this amendment says that no state shall "deprive any person of life, liberty, or property, without due process of law." Field extends the reach of "liberty" and "property" to the right of a commercial operator to set prices and terms of service.

avenues for commerce that differed substantially from the earlier era of mercantilism. The new ventures required investments of capital far beyond what was then common for agriculture and mercantile commerce, enlarging the role of banks and the emerging masters of capital.

What took public regulation into uncharted legal territory, however, was that the services provided by many of these ventures were entirely new. Early demand for electric lighting, for instance, was highly elastic because candles and gas lamps were still widely used. The value of these enterprises to those who bought them depended less on what they could do at the time and more on what these new capital-intensive technologies made possible in the future. The potential for long-term economic productivity meant that early adopters could gain a competitive advantage over their rivals.

Among its other effects, capitalism magnified the public consequences of economic scale. An ever-increasing share of the economy became dependent on the successful movement of capital. As the movement of this capital began to coalesce into macroeconomic patterns of savings and investment, the consequences of failure, incompetence, and chicanery began to ripple far beyond the private interests that caused them. This challenged some of the premises and mechanisms of commercial regulation that had existed up to that time.

All of this meant that when the concept of "utility" began to evolve after the American Civil War, there were few guiding principles and little precedent for addressing the new public interest issues that arose. The social contract abstractions that grew out of the Enlightenment found themselves in the crucible of an economic reality that was far more dynamic than the placid environment in which these concepts were first theorized. "Know it when you see it" was no longer a sufficient approach to defining monopoly. Sorting out just how such an enterprise was "affected with a public interest" became complicated because economic activity grew more complex, specialized, and interdependent. Indeed, this can be considered the turning point at which utilities began to emerge as the economic entities we know today.

The new enterprises added a peculiar twist to the debate between Chief Justice Waite and Justice Field in *Munn v. Illinois*. Those who held close control over a new technology often sought extra protection from the State—preserving secret processes, shutting out competition by establishing exclusive franchises, appropriating public lands for private use, and encroaching on individual property rights for the sake of the public interest.

The potential for profit and the absence of useful regulatory precedent opened the door to *ad hoc*, unchecked, and highly pathological relationships between the emerging utilities, city government, and the political machinery that affected the fortunes of both. City electric works in Philadelphia, New York, and other cities in the late 19th century became enmeshed (not unwillingly) in patronage networks. Natural monopoly and the municipal franchise kept the firms themselves insulated from competition, but the jobs provided by the utility had political value to the mayors, aldermen, and operatives who had a hand in protecting the utility's exclusive service franchise. The link between protected paychecks and protected votes in local elections benefitted all the business and political players who were engaged in the tight network of electric and political power.[13]

Writing in 1912 for the U.S. National Municipal League, Clyde King observed that "There is no sidestepping the fact that, in American cities, municipal utilities are too often the city's actual governing power." He describes a compelling and often replicated story of economic power and administrative inexperience. Unlike managing roads and ports, operating power plants and delivering power to customers safely required detailed

---

[13] Clyde King, ed., *The Regulation of Municipal Utilities* (New York: D. Appleton and Co., 1912), p. 20.

knowledge of a new technology based on a young science. The few who had learned it were needed in the business itself. Those left with figuring out how this new enterprise intersected the public interest could only turn to the enterprise itself for knowledge about how to regulate it—a knowledge vacuum easily filled by opportunism and cronyism.

The Question of Monopoly

The line between public interest and private interest—and, therefore, public utility and private enterprise—has grown more convoluted. The "know it when you see it" method used by kings under common law to define monopoly must be replaced with more rigorous defining criteria. To do that, it is still worthwhile to consult the public interest compass used in *Munn v Illinois*.

If British common law had written down the rationale for declaring an enterprise to be a public monopoly, the key principles might have included these:

- It is impossible, impractical, uneconomic, or inconvenient to society for more than one enterprise to provide the service.
- The service in question is indispensable and non-substitutable across the economy.
- Discriminatory access (that is, capriciously allowing some people access to the service and denying it to others) puts those who do not have access at a systematic, material, and unfair disadvantage.
- Making the service universally available is not something the private sector would seek to achieve if left on its own.

Economic definitions of monopoly often emphasize the relative efficiency of a single-supplier versus multiple suppliers. A natural monopoly is such that if a theoretical second supplier were to enter the market for providing a good, the total cost of producing any amount of the good would be higher than if a single supplier were to produce the same amount of the good.

Pure economic definitions do not sufficiently reach all the public interest nuances of monopoly, however. For example, if the goods in question are not essential to most economic activity, society may care little whether the niche demand is satisfied by one supplier or several. For goods that are universally or near-universally essential, however, cost-induced limitations could matter significantly. Electricity is a prime example. Lack of access reduces economic efficiency, imposes limits and hardship on personal lifestyle choices, and increases social disparity between those who have electric access and those who do not. These consequences have ramifications for the public interest. In order for the benefits of electricity to be spread as equitably as possible, costs need to be as low as possible. However, a monopoly enterprise does not tend to keep costs low unless compelled through regulation.[14]

It is useful to distinguish between *natural* monopoly and *virtual* monopoly (the term used in *Munn v Illinois*). These are not really two different types of monopoly; they represent a continuum of causes. Natural monopoly describes conditions where supply is constrained by the impossibility of a second supplier making the investments and preparations necessary to provide a good or service currently being provided by the incumbent. Geographic limitations, the public inconvenience of having more than one network of physically imposing infrastructure in the same area, or a customer base that is too small to provide enough sales to support a new market entrant's capital and set-up costs can create a natural monopoly.

A monopoly may be *virtual* if factors other than nature result in supply and demand conditions that make new investment just as unprofitable as it would be under a natural monopoly. Consider a monopolist whose capital investments were subsi-

---

[14] A monopolist's natural economic inclination is to raise prices up to, but not higher than, the point that consumers would turn away in numbers so large that the monopolist's revenues would start to fall.

dized or enjoyed some other form of protection under the regulatory contract in the past. These protections reduced the monopolist's cost of capital, thereby reducing both its cost of producing a good and the prices it charged the public. If a potential new market entrant cannot beat the monopolist's subsidized price—but could have beaten an unsubsidized price—the monopoly will be effective by virtue of the exclusive protection the monopolist continues to enjoy.

The key point is this: *The public interest changes if monopoly is no longer natural and if the conditions that sustain a virtual monopoly dissolve.* More than any single technological change, this is the socioeconomic force that is bringing the utility of the future into being and putting existential stress on old regulatory institutions.

The dissolution of monopoly conditions means that the electric sector must replace one set of public interest objectives with another. The new public interest objectives may be understood as the conditions needed to achieve more social benefits, with less cost. These new objectives refocus the public interest on two areas: choice and competition. Both choice and competition are becoming more feasible in some parts of the electricity sector's supply chain, which has public interest ramifications that are particularly relevant to the utility of the future.

For now, I set aside questions of implementation. Poor execution of a good idea poses a different set of questions, and these will be addressed in later chapters. The discussion in this chapter focuses strictly on the ideals behind competition and choice, the public interests at stake, and the ethical consequences of obstructing either.

Customer Choice

The ability to exercise consumer choice is the economic analogue of political liberty. Just as the exercise of free speech and a free press can encourage a higher level of public discourse, consumer freedom can encourage better service in the marketplace.

Consumer preferences can be very diverse. This is why restaurants have menus, car dealers have showrooms, department stores have display racks, and real estate agents participate in large listing services. Most people will prefer some combination of steak and potatoes, not just steak or potatoes. Imagine, however, the selection of one point on the spectrum of preferences—one combination of steak and potatoes that will serve as the universal portion of steak and the universal portion of potatoes. Only the people who are already on this part of the steak-to-potato preference spectrum will be happy. All others will be relatively less satisfied, with individual happiness decreasing most among those who want nothing but steak or nothing but potatoes.

Earlier I set out two frameworks for thinking about the public interest: teleological and deontological. Lack of customer choice fails both tests. Under utilitarianism's teleological standard, which is based on maximizing aggregate happiness across society, moving from choice to the lack of choice would create a reduction in total happiness. Those who already like steak and potatoes in the proportion that has been selected as the universal standard will be indifferent; everyone else will be less happy. The natural social optimum—maximum satisfaction of total happiness—would be realized in a system that allowed each individual to mix steak and potatoes to their own taste.

At the same time, the standard portion fails the deontological test. Recall Kant's Categorical Imperative: An action is good only if anyone could step into anyone else' shoes and find the change reasonable and agreeable. Assume in this example that policy stipulates one steak-to-potatoes ratio applicable to everybody. This standard ratio interacts with each individual's preference for steak and potatoes, which varies across the population. Only for one subset of society would the encounter between preference and standard be agreeable. Everyone else would be required to forego their preferences. The benefit of the change, therefore, would not be universal.

Consequently, choice is the default condition favored by the public interest. Whether retail electricity service is comparable to steak and potatoes depends on several factors that will be explored in later chapters. Certainly, a major consideration is the degree to which choice is affected by institutions—particularly laws, regulatory precedent, and utility practices—which themselves are an outcome of earlier interpretations of the public interest. These institutional constraints can be independent of what is technologically possible and economically realistic. The point here is that choice is in the public interest.

For most of the electric sector's regulated history, "choice" has been rudimentary: to take electricity service or not. As the economy has become more dependent on electricity—either as a necessary input to economic production or as a basic lifestyle necessity—the practicality of choosing "not" has all but vanished. Economists describe this as an increasing inelasticity of demand: Options for doing without the good, or for substituting it with something else, are increasingly limited. This growing inelasticity of demand for electricity heightened the need for regulatory oversight of the monopoly.

Utility practice has been to regard customers as generic points of consumption: modeled the same, served the same, and charged the same. This is still common in electricity service markets that are dominated by monopoly providers. A single rate and common terms of service for each customer's category (residential, commercial, industrial) is the hallmark of this old model of social standardization.[15] As long as customers behave the

---

[15] Utility tariff books have long differentiated industrial and commercial customers by the voltage level of service required. Within these rather coarse delineations (often labeled "small commercial" or "large commercial"), the same rate formula applies. Rates for residential customers were not similarly divided, as service was almost always at a low voltage level.

same way, this model of doing business provides enough stability for the utility and its regulators to assign all the costs of providing electricity service.

The problem is that customers no longer behave the same. Some of the factors that differ across customers include:

- *Cost vs. reliability.* Some customers can make do with a lower level of reliability, especially if the cost is lower. Others need an extra level of reliability and are willing to pay for it.

- *Green power vs. conventional.* Some customers are willing to pay extra to have their electric service sourced solely from renewable resources. Moreover, the economics of that choice are becoming more attractive. Large-scale wind and solar power are converging in cost with newly built conventional generation, and utilities are learning how to integrate renewables into their total supply portfolios more cost effectively.[16]

- *Smart management vs. convenience.* This is an emerging area of choice and diversity. Once utilities send the right price signals, customers with advanced meters (so-called "smart" meters) can adapt their electric usage in ways that reduce their own bills and the utility's cost of providing power. Smart management demands more of the customer. Consequently, some will be eager to embrace smart management, while others will value the convenience of keeping things simple.

All three of these choices are discussed elsewhere in this book. There, I will consider the technical bounds and economic consequences of all these choices, as well as the need to ensure customer rates provide sufficient price signals to reward cost-saving behavior and to penalize cost-causing behavior. The question

---

[16] Cost effectiveness for wind power and solar power also depend on siting the generation equipment in areas with an abundance of those raw resources.

here is whether the *ability* to make such choices is in the public interest. Or to flip the proposition: Does it run counter to the public interest to deny an individual the ability to exercise a choice they judge to be reasonable and beneficial?

Certainly, choice does need reasonable bounds. Even if technologically possible and economically realistic, some extreme choices could be reined in for other public interest reasons. Choices that would harm or violate the rights of others would work against the public interest, even within a broader framework of retail choice. Freedom of speech does not sanction slander or fraud, nor does freedom of religion sanction hate crimes against minorities. Similarly, the public interest does not extend to choices made without regard for harm to the environment or to systemwide reliability. A choice should not deliberately harm society.

The electric sector has taken its first steps toward retail choice; in some markets, these steps have matured into long strides. One of the first modifications to the one-rate-fits-all model was the introduction of consumption tiers in residential rates. This involves charging customers a base rate for each kilowatt-hour consumed per month up to a threshold. All kilowatt-hours consumed beyond that threshold are charged at a higher rate. This was the first attempt at encouraging energy efficiency through rates. It came about at a time when personal lifestyles were becoming more electricity-intensive, especially among the wealthy and the middle class. Central air conditioning, electric appliances, and entertainment all contributed to more megawatt-hours of electricity being consumed per person. Tiered rates provided a choice of sorts—not with respect to the type of electricity service but based instead on a customer's lifestyle choices. An energy-conserving lifestyle could result in lower bills.

The electricity sector has taken other steps towards choice. Tiered rates have become more sophisticated. Many customers are opting to allow the utility limited control of their air conditioners for load management in return for lower utility bills. In retail markets where choice has advanced significantly, customers can choose different pricing schemes that reward use when the cost of producing power is low. This expansion of choice reflects a diversity of economic preferences. If the preferences are diverse—as they certainly seem to be—then the question for the public interest is how choice should be fostered.

Competition

If monopoly conditions of an enterprise recede and competition becomes practical, then the regulation of that enterprise in the public interest also changes.

Before I take up the public interest ramifications of competition, however, a key clarification of terms is necessary. There is a widely held and widely disseminated misunderstanding that "competition" and "deregulation" are synonymous. In Chapter 6 I will explain in detail why this is nonsense. For now, the task is to lay this distracting error aside before proceeding any further, because it can lead to egregious misunderstandings about how to formulate the public interest with regard to the utility of the future.

Market competition is in the public interest; deregulation is not. Deregulation with no competition leads to what is arguably the worse of all possible economic worlds: unregulated oligopoly, in which a handful of companies collude to control prices and prevent others from entering the market. What makes deregulation good or bad is the presence of true competition, which is why this exploration of the public interest focuses there and not on deregulation.[17]

Genuine market competition brings two types of public interest benefits. One is greater economic efficiency. Price-based competition by way of auctions and open-season solicitations generally results in achieving comparable economic value at less cost. This obviously benefits the buyer's private interest, but more germane to this discussion is the public benefit. If the economic environment is conducive to open and robust competition, society overall does a better job of husbanding its collective wealth and natural resources. Productivity tends to be higher, which in turn supports higher wages generally. To the extent that social well-being can be measured by expanded wealth and the conservation of the natural resources used to build that wealth, greater economic competition meets the teleological test of the public interest.

Another major public interest benefit of competition is the encouragement of entrepreneurial innovation. The ability to choose one supplier over another in an open marketplace tends to incentivize creativity and penalize complacency. Innovation might focus on reducing supply chain and production costs, thereby enabling the supplier to reduce costs to the customer. It might focus on better customer service, reduced risk, less price volatility, or the use of environmentally friendly technology and processes. No two customers will balance all these preferences in the same way. The dynamics of choice are examined in more depth later in this book. The point here is that competition stim-

---

[17] By asserting that competition is in the public interest, I also mean that the obverse is true: "pantomime" or false competition is harmful to the public interest if not regulated. As I will explain in Chapter 6, one of the new responsibilities of the regulator in the utility of the future is to monitor market conditions to ensure competition is fair and undistorted by market power. If the State cannot ensure competitive fairness, then the public interest is better served by continued regulation.

ulates innovation in a way that the monopoly utility business model cannot replicate.

Socially beneficial competition is not a laissez-faire free-for-all, however. This is apparent by looking at the possible effects of pure laissez faire economics. A downward slide into a predatory market where cheating and coercion control individual economic decisions would fail virtually all public interest tests. Economic decisions would not be based on increasing welfare. They would be defensive in that many (paying a bribe, for example) would aim to deflect harm rather than to increase happiness. Drug cartels and other forms of organized crime are examples of laissez faire taken to sociopathic extremes.

Not all possible weak-state outcomes are this dire. But because the laissez faire model has no inherent way to rule out this scenario, the recipe for socially beneficial competition must lie elsewhere. This suggests that the public interest (and therefore the State's role) does not go away when moving toward competition. But it does change. The State's focus shifts away from economic decisions themselves and toward the conditions in the economic environment in which decisions are made privately. Its concern becomes whether consumers have practical options for increasing well-being as they define it themselves and whether the market is open to all providers who believe they can do a better job meeting those preferences.

Competition in the marketplace should be open and it should be fair. Open access means that no incumbent competitor should have the power to prevent a potential market entrant from acquiring the capital (human as well as financial) to provide services to willing buyers. Nor should an incumbent be able to exert undue political or regulatory influence that would prevent an otherwise qualified provider from setting up shop. Market entry would still depend on the newcomer's business ability, existing market conditions, and the innovation and service the newcomer could offer customers.

The public's interest in a well-ordered economy would migrate toward universally applicable rules of conduct rather than setting specific prices or approving procurements. The State would become a "market cop" of sorts, ensuring that the rules of the market were fair and prosecuting those who step outside the bounds of those rules.

These conditions are in the public interest deontologically because they would benefit any person who seeks to enter the market, with no systematic exception. They also make possible a teleological increase in total satisfaction across society (presuming that choices to take advantage of new competition increase individual satisfaction by increasing benefits, reducing costs, or both).

Case Study: Holding Companies and the Great Depression

Some of the electric sector's early growing pains illustrate how the public interest can suffer when the regulatory contract is circumvented and the chastening hand of competition is absent. A public interest crisis emerged in the early part of the 20th century caused by the expansion of trusts and utility holding companies. A feeding-frenzy of windfall profit-seeking ensued, contributing to the stock market crash of 1929 and the Great Depression that followed.

The problem posed by holding companies was their ability to mingle assets of utilities from different states, putting crucial regulatory issues constitutionally out of the reach of state and local governments while at the same time preserving the utility's effective monopoly status. The Supreme Court affirmed the constitutional limitation posed by the Interstate Commerce Clause even though, as a practical matter, there was no federal authority that was ready to step into this regulatory void.[18] Local operating companies still provided electricity to customers under protected

---

[18]*Smith v. Illinois Bell Telephone Co.*, 282 U.S. 133 (1930).

monopoly franchises granted by local and state governments, but by 1929 more than 80% of the country's electric generating capacity was in the hands of thirteen interstate holding companies. Local control of a regulated utility and its costs thus grew to be an illusion.

The Federal Trade Commission spent more than seven years investigating the utility holding company phenomenon. Its 1935 report to Congress summarized two broad categories of abuse, both of which serve to illustrate the role of competition as an element of the public interest. One category of abuse was what the FTC described as the "milking of operating companies" by their parent holding companies. This involved the holding company requiring the local operating company to obtain services for power plant maintenance, engineering, equipment procurement, and other parts of the business from holding company affiliates. These contracts were not competed and were sometimes overpriced by as much as 300%.

Competition in an operating utility's procurement of service contracts would have increased economic efficiency—or in teleological terms, would have resulted in more collective good with less application of social wealth. Exclusive service contracts eliminated the possibility of substituting one service provider with another in order to get a better price. This did not pose a problem to the utility itself, however, because under the regulatory contract such operating costs were simply passed through to customer rates. Profit margins didn't increase for the operating company but they did for the holding company, which was beyond the regulatory reach of local authorities. This robbed customers of potential savings and squandered wealth that otherwise could have been put to economically productive use.

This direct harm—less economic efficiency—also provided financial grease for the second and more devastating category of abuse cited by the FTC: the leveraging of ownership, stock, and indebtedness. A small ownership share in a local utility (often much less than 50%) combined with proxies from other linked ownerships and the issuance of non-voting stock was enough to give the holding company effective control over a utility beyond the reach of the local or state regulatory body. This same leveraging tactic was often used to bind smaller holding companies into larger holding companies, sometimes with as much as six levels of leveraged ownership. Samuel Insull, a protégé of Thomas Edison who began consolidating electric companies in Chicago shortly after the turn of the century, had by 1930 leveraged a $27 million equity position into control of half a billion dollars in assets spanning thirty-two states.

Holding companies were not in competition with one another, because the customer bases that provided the infusion of revenue for the associated operating companies never overlapped. Each operating company was a bona fide, franchised monopoly. If a holding company required an operating company in one state to use a service contract that was overpriced by 300%, the costs would be passed on to local customers who would not have the ability to switch to a supplier in a neighboring state where rates did not carry such a pass-through. This sweetened the incentive for pyramiding to the extent that thousands of small investors were happy to buy non-voting shares of holding company common stock.[19]

Earlier laws such as the Sherman Antitrust Act of 1890 provided the federal government with some limited legal basis for mitigating this public interest gap. But interstate utility holding companies posed a new problem that went beyond the oil, tobacco, and steel industries whose anticompetitive practices brought the Sherman Act into being. Generating electricity was, at that time, a natural monopoly that was becoming increasingly important to the economic growth of the country. The industry's central role meant that no intricate trust machinations were needed to commandeer a monopoly market position (as in the steel and oil industries). Monopoly was already a natural part of the business.

The utility holding company web began a financial free-fall in 1929. By 1936, fifty-three holding companies with an aggregate $1.7 billion in assets—about $30 billion in 2017 dollars—were in receivership. In 1935, Congress enacted a targeted remedy in the form of the Public Utilities Holding Company Act (PUHCA). The law imposed a heavy regulatory hand on the operation of holding companies, to the extent that by the end of

---

[19] The FTC's findings speak directly to how holding companies abrogated the regulatory contract, and are worth quoting at length:

> The holding company, as such, performs no producing function. For that reason, in the utility field it has not been treated as a utility company and therefore has not been subject to regulations as such. Is it usually subject to no regulation or control whatever. Operating utilities are the companies to which the Commonwealths have granted the charters to perform a general public utility service. These grants imply and definitely impose reciprocal duties, but as a result of holding-company control and management, many operating companies, under the compulsion of holding-company control, have contracted away the real performance of their principal charter functions to the holding company or to other companies designated by the holding company, thus leaving only a hollow corporate shell within the jurisdiction of the State where the operating company does business. The entire holding-company problem has grown up under the enactment of statutes which abrogated the common-law rule which forbade one corporation to acquire and own stock in another.

World War II most of them had been broken up and those that remained were no more than one ownership level away from their respective operating companies.

The question here, however, is whether competition could have provided the ounce of prevention that would have avoided the need for PUHCA's draconian cure. We may never know for sure, but the question itself is a lesson for anyone hoping to understand tomorrow's electric utility paradigm. Competing service contracts certainly would have brought greater operational efficiency (and savings for customers). This would have removed some of the economic sweetener that encouraged holding companies to build highly leveraged ownership pyramids. This appearance of easy money proved too tempting to investors, who were happy to take non-voting shares of common stock and leave the decisions to the preferred shareholders who had engineered the pyramid.

Interdependence and the Public Interest

Partly because the world is becoming more complex, and partly because we know so much more about it, segregating the effects of different types of human activity into separate public interest spheres is becoming more problematic, less reasonable, and less honest. Things that once could be analyzed and understood solely within their own domains are becoming increasingly dependent on what happens outside their spheres of activity.

Advances in physics and other sciences have made us increasingly aware of the interdependence of all things. This interdependence has consequences for just about any ethics framing the public interest.

Recall the traditional public interest balance for regulating electric utilities offered at the beginning of this chapter: least cost, greatest reliability. Both these values are entirely contained within the realm of the power sector. They involve decisions about capital investment and system operation made within the power sector and paid for entirely by the customers who use the system. But the technologies used to generate power have effects that are not recorded in a utility's standard system of accounting. Burning coal results in air emissions; nuclear power produces radioactive waste that must be managed and disposed of carefully; extracting and moving natural gas entails methane emissions; and even renewable technologies involve some life cycle cost in their manufacture.

Many of these interdependencies have shadow consequences that economists refer to as "externalities." For most of the electricity sector's economic history, externalities fell outside the public interest sphere of electric utilities. If the public interest is to be truly upheld, however, these indirect effects must be considered—especially as society becomes more electricity-intensive.

In economics, the presence of externalities means that an action involving capital, labor, technology, revenue, and other common economic variables can create costs (or even benefits) that are outside the immediate decision or process being modeled. More sophisticated economic analysis will attempt to internalize externalities by monetizing their effects, but in many cases the impacts are not easily monetized. Health impacts and mortality, for example, are often monetized based on lost earnings power, but both have emotional and social consequences far beyond the earning power of the individual who may be affected.

The concern at hand in this chapter, however, is not the economics of measuring externalities. The initial question with respect to the public interest is the rationale for taking these interdependencies into account at all. Taking them into account means more than giving them an inconsequential nod and then carrying on as though they never happened. It means putting them on the table at the beginning of the decision process, investigating them with the same thoroughness given to other issues, and giving them sufficient weight to change a public action if warranted by the evidence.[20]

Not everything that the electricity sector does inflicts the same magnitude of harm in the world outside the sector, but in many cases the consequences are widespread enough to warrant scrutiny. Access to water, for example, is commonly held to be in the public interest. Therefore, producing an otherwise economically beneficial good or service in a way that incidentally pollutes public water supplies to the point that they are unfit for human consumption would be a public interest concern. This would be true regardless of how the impact occurs, whether directly through an accidental waste spill, or indirectly by exacerbating the likelihood of drought. The fact that the causal action was at one time approved by a regulator who had a much narrower view of the public interest does not mitigate the actual harm to the environment and public health, even if unintended or unforeseen by the regulator at the time the decision was made.

Interdependencies by their nature involve disparate perspectives and conflicting interests that are linked by organic pathways difficult to compartmentalize through analysis. These interests differ in power, economic status, and even awareness. An important point for the public interest is that in most cases, it is beyond the capability of any of these single interests to reconcile the entire body of interests in a way that minimizes total harm or that maximizes total social good. Because each interest in this network of different processes has its own framework and values, arbitration of all interests is skewed if doing it is left to only one or two interests.

Not every internalized externality will change the economic equation. Not every non-monetized externality is compelling

---

[20] For example, the National Environmental Policy Act requires an environmental impact study if a potential action by a federal agency could have harmful consequences on wildlife habitat, air quality, water resources, or cultural treasures. Federal actions have been struck down in court because the environmental studies insufficiently addressed relevant externalities.

enough to change the nature of the public interest. Yet, to presume at the outset that they do not count is simplistic and leads to serious ethical failure. Consider acid rain. The balance between costs and benefits swings more towards building a coal plant if sulfur dioxide emissions are ignored and scrubbers are not included in capital costs. However, the resulting higher acidity of natural water supplies can affect the yield of agriculture and aquaculture, worsen public health, and impose costs elsewhere in the economy. Non-monetized externalities can include loss of species and degraded recreational value of natural spaces. Yet when most of today's large coal-fired generators were approved in the 1960s and 1970s, these externalities seldom entered into decision-makers' conception of the public interest. Even if they did, it was not with the same weight given to low electricity rates and high system reliability.

Today we know what many of those impacts are, and we recognize their effect on the public interest. Moreover, there comes a point at which decision makers can see an externality's effect on the public interest, even if the mechanics of those impacts are not completely understood. This is particularly relevant to the generation of electricity and its associated impact on climate change. *Whether* human activity contributes to carbon-loading in the atmosphere is no longer a serious scientific question. *How* and *how much* are the current research questions, and the body of knowledge is increasing. But it is not necessary to wait for a complete library of findings to know that there is (and will continue to be) a public interest at stake.

Every potential consequence of global warming has both an economic impact and a likelihood that it will occur. Insurance companies and economists call this an *expected value*: the cost that one case of lung cancer can inflict on an individual and society, adjusted by the probability that the policy holder might develop lung cancer. The cost of an anti-smoking program is measured against the expected value of fewer cases of lung cancer. Likewise, every potential impact of global warming—longer and more severe drought, gradual inundation of low-lying islands and coastal areas, and other climate-related damages—has an expected value.

Recognizing and acting on the public interest does not mean waiting for scientific experts to provide certainty.[21] It means comparing the expected value of global warming's consequences with the range of options for doing something about it. Good policy, therefore, acts on the options that cost the least but do the most towards reducing the probability of severe consequences due to climate change. For example, a wide range of options are available for reducing the consumption of electricity through greater energy efficiency (thus reducing generation and emissions from coal and natural gas plants). These options can be ordered from least expensive to most expensive, enabling regulators, utilities, and the public to assess how much efficiency could be achieved at the least cost. Options for making renewable energy a larger part of the generation mix can be examined in a similar manner.[22]

---

[21] As anyone who didn't sleep through their science classes would know, science does not operate on certainty; it operates on probability. Experiments are designed to winnow down the number of possible explanations for an observed phenomenon to the one with the highest probability of being replicable. A team of researchers intent on precision might report that their results have a 99% chance of explaining a phenomenon—not "certain" in the strictest sense, but consistent enough to be reasonably useful. The fact that many of these same scientists are also parents and grandparents is why so many of them are worried about how public decisions might affect the phenomena they've studied, even if the probability of harmful outcomes falls short of the (never-attained) 100% statistical benchmark.

[22] Options at the least-cost ends of the supply curves for energy efficiency and renewable energy can be economically compelling even without considering their environmental benefits. For example, efficiency that reduces peak system load can defer or even eliminate the need for costly new investments in peaking capacity. Recent declines in renewable energy costs mean that adding a well-sited wind or solar project to the generation portfolio can reduce exposure to fuel price fluctuations that constitute an uncertainty for natural gas generators in the portfolio, resulting in total costs that are both low and stable.

An important yet complicating aspect of public interest interdependencies is that they span time as well as space. Most of the nation's fleet of large supercritical steam power plants were built before society even recognized that emissions were an environmental problem. Siting, supply, and design decisions made in the 1960s were based on cost, with relatively little consideration for long-term impacts on the local and global natural environment. Had society known then what it knows now, many of those decisions might very well have been different. The fact is, however, that the State—embodied in the decision makers of the time—had insufficient understanding of the interdependencies at work. The result is a huge number of "sunk" investments that cannot be un-invested without incurring a different set of severe social impacts.

A decision made in the past might very well fail the test of public interest today, but correcting it might also be ethically complicated if the fix entails a new set of harms. Consequently, evaluating the public interest ramifications of correcting a past decision cannot be done by applying today's values to yesterday's circumstances. Take the example of a large coal-fired power plant built in an economically impoverished part of the country decades ago, and that has come to provide most of the area's highest-paying jobs. The public interest has changed so that if the same plant were proposed today, its approval would be extremely unlikely. Yet it was built and is now a pivotal component of a fragile regional economy not diversified enough to replace the jobs that would be lost. On one side of the public interest equation are questions of environmental impact. On the other side are concerns about the economic disruption that would occur to a vulnerable population. Just as dismissing the interdependent environmental consequences would fail today's tests of the public interest, so too would dismissing the interdependencies that have grown over time and that would lead to economic disruption. An ethical weighing of the public interest would need to find the solution that best reconciles both issues without ignoring either.

Sometimes the new knowledge is compelling enough to justify a change in direction even if the cost is high. When nuclear power was being promoted in the 1960s and 1970s, it was often described as a source of electricity that would be "too cheap to meter." That theme all but disappeared in 1979 when multiple failures in the cooling system almost led to a melt-down in one of the reactor cores at the newly commissioned Three-Mile Island nuclear plant near Harrisburg, Pennsylvania. Clean-up and repairs amounted to more than $1 billion (in 2017 dollars, more than $2 billion). Just as significant were the design modifications that regulators began to require in nuclear plants that were currently under construction. Utility regulators had to rethink major capital decisions. Should they cancel a nuclear project and write off the sunk costs as a loss? Should they authorize design revisions and increase customer rates to cover them? Either way, the result was that this "too cheap to meter" power often caused major increases in the rates end-use customers had to pay for electricity.

Ignoring a significant externality out-of-hand can fail both teleological and deontological public interest tests. For example, consider a proposed coal plant whose operation would create economic losses for the surrounding community due to diminished agricultural yields. If the decision to build changes depending on whether the utility can keep those costs off its balance sheet, building the plant would fail Kant's categorical imperative by creating a double-standard dilemma: the cost would be unacceptable if the utility itself had to bear it, but would be acceptable if the utility could make others pay for it. Environmental justice concerns might add another layer of deontological hazard. For example, if the plant were located near an economically vulnerable population, the environmental impacts would fall hardest on these individuals and less on affluent customers separated from the plant by miles of high-voltage transmission. If the neighborhood environmental degradation would not be acceptable to affluent customers if they themselves were to feel those impacts, the deontological standard for the public interest would not be met. Sweeping a dirty environment under someone else's carpet fails the deontological test of the public interest on its face.

Interdependencies also place more of a burden on Mill's utilitarian standard for increasing the sum of benefits. A wider scope increases the elements that must be included in the equation by which social happiness is summed. While one cannot say a priori that this pushes the scale into negative values, it does require that additional elements be considered when evaluating the public interest.

As with cost and reliability, the public interest regarding the natural environment and other points outside the electric sector is a balance. Completely eliminating human-caused harm to the natural environment is impossible. But no reasonable understanding of the public interest would call for perfect reliability (too expensive) or for electricity that was free (too unreliable). Similarly, minimizing harm to the natural environment is reconciled in the context of other aims.

Beyond the Empirical

There is, besides all these other reasons, a spiritual rationale for taking interdependencies into account.

Interdependence—or to be precise, *interconnectedness*—also brings the transcendence of human experience into the realm of the public interest. The two terms—interdependence and interconnectedness—align but are not identical. Interdependence speaks to the mechanics of processes. Specifically, it refers to processes working as a complex network of causes and effects. Any given effect—survival, happiness, a bountiful harvest—*depends* on disparate causes, with each cause itself being an effect that depends on another set of disparate causes. Interconnectedness is somewhat different. It is a characteristic of being that exists even when the mechanics of interdependence are at rest—the epistemological "why" that underlies interdependence. As such, interconnectedness is a characteristic of nature that speaks to human meaning, which resides not with the individual member but in the relationship between the individual and the universal whole.

Interconnectedness is also where consciousness enters the picture: the ineffable but very real sense of belonging that a person has with family or with tribe; the instinct connecting a bird with its environment, saying when it is time to nest and when it is time to fly from one continent to another. It is why we intuit that there is something to life that is greater than ourselves. Interconnectedness means that "just as you did it to one of the least of these who are members of my family, you did it to me."[23]

The idea of interconnectedness as a spiritual attribute of the world and human existence is by no means exclusive to the Abrahamic religions. Hindu and Buddhist traditions represent interconnectedness as a jeweled net thrown by the deity Indra. Each jewel in the net reflects the light of every other, thus the universe arises, diversifies, and evolves as a cosmic choreography of interbeing woven into an expansive web of causes and effects. Consequentially, says Buddhist teacher Thich Nhat Hahn, "everything in the cosmos has come together to bring us to this table." Seeing interconnectedness in the world lays bare all the workings of cause and effect, so that through mindfulness and

---

[23] Matt. 25:40 (NRSV). An important question to ponder about this passage is whether Jesus is simply referring to himself as a person, or is instead using himself as a representation of the divinity resident in all creation. My own view is that the former interpretation is too self-serving to comport with the rest of the New Testament. Applying the latter interpretation, a universal practice of compassion, selflessness, and mindfulness cultivates the quality of consciousness Jesus exhorted his followers to develop in themselves, which would enable them to "inherit the kingdom prepared for you from the foundation of the world" (25:34).

right action individuals can create their own destinies and thus achieve liberation. This, according to the Upanishads, is spiritual fearlessness: "He who sees everywhere the Self in all existences and all existences in the Self, shrinks not thereafter from aught."[24]

Consciousness varies by the amount of space-time it can apprehend. Thus, while animal, human, and supra-human or divine consciousness may be connected on the same spectrum of experience, the connections are not felt with the same clarity or intensity by everyone. Nor are the connections interpreted the same way. But that really does not matter, especially with respect to the public interest. Faith and reason both lead to the conclusion that each human being is part of a universal whole that comprises networks of interconnected and overlapping networks. This interconnection carries with it a duty for mindfulness and respect for what Daly and Cobb describe as a "community of communities," enfolding realms large and small, human and natural, visible and invisible.[25] Topically focused decisions such as those affecting the creation and use of electricity have the capacity to resonate throughout this network of communities.

Therefore, if policy decisions are to point society in the direction of our most spiritually exalted humanity and not away from it, they ought to begin from a sense of reverence that expands beyond one single sphere of human activity. Interconnectedness is an attribute of being human that leads to the interdependence of our actions and well-being. It is the interconnection between human activities and the natural world that make the deontological and teleological inseparable measures of the public interest. The interconnectedness of being across space and

---

[24] See Thich Nhat Hahn, *The Heart of the Buddha's Teaching* (Berkeley, CA: Parallax Press, 1998). The translation of the Isha Upanishad used here is from Sri Aurobindo, *The Complete Works of Sri Aurobindo* (Pondicherry, India: Sri Aurobindo Ashram trust, 2003).

[25] Daly and Cobb, *For the Common Good* (*supra* at note 8).

time teleologically means that each individual has inherent worth and dignity deontologically: Each is part of the complex spiritual fabric of the universe.

Of course, there will always be those who persist in denying the moral and spiritual implications of human interdependence with the natural world. But evolution will not halt for the stubbornness of a few. If social decisions are to be evolutionary, they need to embrace the interconnectedness of the real world.

Restating the Public Interest

With the foregoing in mind, I propose the following restatement of the public interest to guide future electric utility regulation.

It is in the public interest for society to enjoy the benefits of electric power at the least cost with the greatest reliability *and produced with the least harmful impact on the natural environment. Access to these benefits should be equitable, should accommodate customer diversity, and should not unjustly shift the burden of costs to those who do not cause them. Furthermore, if any aspect of electricity production or delivery can be accomplished without the protection of a monopoly franchise, competition in the provision of such service should be open, fair, and sufficiently robust that no individual provider or collusion of providers can control the market price of their services.*

All of the points included in this restatement are beneficial across all members of society, and they lead to a higher level of happiness for society. They therefore pass both public interest tests (teleological and deontological) as described throughout this chapter. Moreover, it is unreasonable to task the private sector with these goals, or even to assume that they will naturally fall out of private sector activity. Individual actions are governed by the microeconomic aim of maximizing *individual* welfare, which is valuable but is not the same as public interest values such as equity and the integrity of the natural environment. Protecting these values are public sector tasks.

As with the traditional public interest values of cost and reliability, this restatement involves balancing values that run in different and at times opposite directions. Like cost and reliability, these component values are not absolute. Society doesn't reject the benefit of electricity simply because it isn't free. Equally nonsensical is to argue that any environmental protection equates to economic shutdown—a common tactic used by many who oppose clean energy technologies.

St. Paul writes: "When I was a child, I spoke as a child, I understood as a child, I thought as a child; but when I became a man, I put away childish things."[26] The public interest for electric utilities has reached a similar coming-of-age. Not only is each new element of this restatement of the public interest attainable, the sector has already begun putting away the old-world view that looks only at cost and reliability. Technological advances are giving utilities, regulators, and customers more insight into the consequences of how electricity is generated and used. Utilities certainly cannot solve social problems outside the bounds of providing electricity, but they can choose investments that avoid making some problems worse. That begins by recognizing the electric sector's place in an interconnection of natural and socioeconomic systems. Interdependence means that decisions made by utilities, regulators, and customers have far-reaching consequences that can now be understood and taken into account.

This restatement of the public interest suggests that electric utilities are not going away. The prophets of doom who point to

---

[26] I Corinthians 13:11 (NRSV). St. Paul writes this in the context of a broader message: that all human actions should be imbued with love. Equity, compassion, and fairness are manifestations of love. The degree to which the public interest manifests these same values indicates the character of the society we pass on to future generations.

utilities' financial "death spiral" are misreading what is really happening. Evolving public interest imperatives are changing what it means to be a utility. This, in turn, means lawmakers and regulators need to rethink what they are regulating—and why. The electric sector's "utility-ness" is changing; it is time to update the regulatory contract.

Chapter 3: The Economics of Creative Destruction

This is a time of disruption in the electricity sector, but it would be a mistake to chalk this up to technology exclusively. In fact, the entire capitalist economy itself is in a never-ending roil of evolution. The living economy is a seething cauldron of changing consumer preferences, new technological possibilities, and redefined interactions between the public and private sectors. Old business models fall and new ones arise, sometimes so completely that once-common implements of the economy can within just a few decades be found only in museums. Thus, rotary telephones gave way to smart phones, typewriters and adding machines gave way to personal computers, and horse-drawn carriages gave way to steam power and automobiles.

Technology is part of the story, but the drama and the trauma are found in the socioeconomic forces that propel the transition. In his seminal work *Capitalism, Socialism, and Democracy*, economist Joseph Schumpeter wrote:

> The fundamental impulse that sets and keeps the capitalist engine in motion comes from the new consumers' goods, the new methods of production or transportation, the new markets, the new forms of industrial organization that capitalist enterprise creates....The opening up of new markets, foreign or domestic, and the organizational development from the craft shop and factory to such concerns as U.S. Steel illustrate the same process of industrial mutation—if I may use that biological term—that incessantly revolutionizes the economic structure from within, incessantly destroying the old one, incessantly creating a new one. This process of Creative Destruction is the essential fact about capitalism.[27]

---

[27] Joseph A. Schumpeter, *Capitalism, Socialism, and Democracy* (New York: Harper Perennial, 1942).

In deconstructing capitalism, Schumpeter was less concerned with capitalism's morality than he was with understanding where its evolutionary path led. I take a similar approach here. One can argue capitalism's virtues and vices until the cows come home, and meanwhile be distracted from the opportunities that are at hand. My concern is with the socioeconomic evolution that is actually happening, and what it means for the electric sector generally and utilities in particular.

Schumpeter's notion of creative destruction is interwoven with the public interest challenges described in the previous chapter, thus it is not unusual for the State to have a hand in the change. A new technology's first stages of development might enjoy some protection from competition, by way of intellectual property protection or some other State franchise for exclusive operation in proscribed market areas. The economic evolution might involve public convenience issues that require the State to weigh new uses of eminent domain against established private property rights. If the evolution is more disruptive to some than to others, the public interest may impel the State to ensure universal or nondiscriminatory access to the new enabling technology. Even if the State is not causing the socioeconomic evolution, the public interest may demand responses to make the transition less disruptive and more socially equitable. Creative destruction and its effects are not solely economic, and the public interest is never indifferent to how it unfolds.[28]

The concern in this chapter is how the public interest affects the process of electric utilities' capital formation when monopoly enterprises are no longer natural monopolies. The public-private intersection took peculiar forms when it came to electric utilities. These peculiarities arose ad hoc as technological advances opened new possibilities. Many vestiges of these improvised capital formation devices continue today and complicate the matter of capital formation for the utility of the future. What economic history makes clear, however, is that the public interest has a legitimate role in making the transition smoother.

Throughout this chapter (and elsewhere in this book) I use the term "gigaplants," which I introduced in the previous chapter. This is not common electricity sector parlance, but it is useful here. Gigaplants are large central generating stations whose nameplate generating capacity is measured in gigawatts rather than megawatts. These leviathans account for nearly half of all U.S. generating capacity, although their number comprises only 5% of all sites where power is generated. Fossil fuels—primarily

---

[28] Economic theory and analysis often fall into a myopic trap: that economic productivity is the ultimate social good. That is not the assumption here. Competitive markets, which play a major role in the economic framework developed in this chapter, are very good at economic efficiency. But they are agnostic about justice, the integrity of the natural environment, and even basic human happiness. Therefore, it is unreasonable to expect that the forces underlying the economic shifts described here are anything other than indifferent to social values that are not realized monetarily. This by no means negates the value of thinking about the world economically. Economic efficiency is socially beneficial so long as it occurs within the bounds of the public interest. The world might not be entirely rational, but economic forces will follow their own internally consistent logic within the commercial space in which they operate. Economic analysis is useful as long as it does not lose sight of its own bounded rationality. Within this space, economic forces are extremely persistent. The State, through regulation, might try to modify economic transformation, but it can neither cause nor stop it. Public policy can let itself be carried by the economic current, attempt to swim upstream of it, or strategically ply the current and navigate it constructively.

coal and natural gas—power more than three fourths of all generating stations larger than one gigawatt, and nearly two-thirds of everything larger than two gigawatts. For most of these plants, capital costs are recovered through the rate bases of the utilities owning shares of the plant. (I will elaborate on rate base shortly.) Here, "gigaplant" refers to a very large generator whose capital costs are recovered through a utility's rate base.[29]

In this story of economic evolution, gigaplants are the brontosauruses. The economic environment is changing in a way that will eventually make these leviathans non-reproducible, if not unsustainable. Creative destruction describes their path to extinction.

This chapter uses Schumpeter's notion of "creative destruction" as a starting point for understanding the economic changes happening today in the electric sector. There are, of course, changes to the general framework that are peculiar to electric utilities. I therefore beg the indulgence of academicians in the field of economic theory; what follows might not be Schumpeterian in the strictest sense, and it is not my purpose for it to be so. The task at hand is to construct an economic framework that describes what is happening in the power sector with enough accuracy and clarity to help decision makers through the fog of uncertainty. My main points are the following:

- *The changes that are happening constitute a true sea change*, not something that is happening simply because of federal or state policy decisions. If anything, "progressive" policy is following the change and adapting to it, not causing it.
- *There is no turning back.* Political attempts to stop the clock of economic evolution risk inflicting significant damage on society.

---

[29] My use of this term excludes large federally funded hydroelectric generation such as Grand Coulee Dam and Hoover Dam in the western United States.

- *Utilities as monopolies will shrink.* They will continue as bundled monopolies only in those parts of the country where economic modernization is slow or where the market is too small to sustain a critical mass of competition.

- *A new role is emerging in the electric sector: the market maker.* Historical utilities are the most likely candidates for taking on this role. Indeed, this new role will define what the "utility of the future" will be. The next two chapters will explain the characteristics of this new function. This chapter sets the groundwork by examining the evolutionary conditions creating the need for a market maker.

The Formation and Use of Capital

One simple question summarizes the problem of capital formation in this era of creative destruction: Would any institutional investor or banker put money into a new coal gigaplant without the protection of the regulatory contract?

One of the most important aspects of creative destruction is how it forces the electric sector to change the way it attracts and applies new capital. Here lurks one of the sector's dirtiest and often forgotten secrets: The legacy gigaplants that constitute such a large part of today's generation fleet only exist because of government-sanctioned subsidies underwritten by the general public. An investment tax credit generated billions of dollars in incentives during the utilities' gigaplant building spree, but that was not what made these big investments possible.[30] More fun-

---

[30] This investment tax credit is not really comparable to the one more recently given to solar and other types of renewable resources. Available for most types of capital investment, it was intended as a general stimulus for a sluggish economy. All types of investments in electric generation took advantage of the credit throughout the 1970s. Thus, while it was indeed a government subsidy, it was not a preferential one.

damental was how utilities took advantage of the regulatory contract to virtually eliminate the risk of an otherwise high-risk capital investment.

This undercuts one of the major criticisms leveled against renewable energy technologies during their commercial takeoff stages—the assertion that tax credits and other financial mechanisms designed to encourage their development distorted market economics. The fatal flaw in these arguments is that they spuriously harken to a pristine economic state that, in fact, did not exist. The gigaplant boom of the 1970s and 1980s relied on an economic environment laced with subsidy and largely insulated from risk. Creative destruction is unraveling these legacy economic conditions.

Acknowledging this truth is important to understanding the utility of the future. It is why, from a basic economic perspective, the utility of the past is never coming back. Before unpacking the economic baggage, however, some introductory points can help make sense of the history of gigaplant capital investment.

First, an old-world utility's profitability did not depend on reducing costs. Set aside, for a moment, the classic economic notion that profit is the difference between revenue and cost. While true for most of the private sector, it has not been true for utilities. A utility's real financial health was a function of something more obscure: the size of its asset base. If the utility's allowed rate of return on its asset base was 8%, its earnings in absolute dollars would increase in step with new capital investments added to the value of its plant in service. One or two new gigaplants could do this nicely. The part of the regulatory contract that made this possible was the utility's return on equity, a key part of any rate case that ensured the utility's ability to attract equity and secure low-cost debt. The greater the value of its total plant-in-service, the greater the returns to shareholders.[31]

Second, the regulators charged with ensuring reasonable rates were often "captured" by the utilities they were supposed to regulate. Setting aside the possibility of corruption, utility rate cases have always been complex affairs. Ever since the early days of electric utilities, the accounting expertise needed to understand the numbers resided mostly with the utility. It was their business after all, and there was no other business like it. Much of a regulatory staffer's early career was often spent learning the arcana that was utility accounting, and on this point, little has changed. Regulatory commission staff have long been—and still are—a fertile recruiting ground for utilities seeking fresh talent that is both highly knowledgeable and grossly underpaid.

Finally, technology enabled the development of gigaplants. Metallurgical advances during and after World War II made it possible to build larger and stronger supercritical boilers. Single units could be built with the capacity to generate 750 megawatts of power or more, due to their ability to use steam at higher temperature and pressure. These large supercritical boilers began to appear in the electric generation fleet in the 1960s, fueled first by coal and natural gas, then by heavy fuel oil in the 1970s, and finally by nuclear power in the 1970s and 1980s. Gigaplants combined two or more of these giant boilers at a single generating station. In the West, many new gigaplants were built near their coal supplies to minimize fuel transportation costs. Transmission, too, was supersized to accommodate the massive injec-

---

[31] Warren Buffett recently described it to Berkshire Hathaway shareholders this way: "Historically, the survival of a local electric company did not depend on its efficiency. In fact, a 'sloppy' operation could do just fine financially…. The joke in the industry was that a utility was the only business that would automatically earn more money by redecorating the boss's office. And some CEOs ran things accordingly." See Berkshire Hathaway's 2015 annual report.

tions of energy. The reductions in line losses that accompanied the extra-high voltage lines also added to the economies of scale.

Traditional Utilities and the Regulatory Contract

The utility's captured customer base was the lifeblood of its capital formation. The monopoly franchise that the regulatory contract provided meant that utility customers had nowhere else to turn to satisfy a demand that was growing and becoming more inelastic.

The regulatory contract did not permit operating expenses to be a profit center for the utility, so all costs of doing business were passed through to customer rates once the State deemed them allowable expenses. That was fine for the utility, however, because the State had already approved the utility's return on equity, which was added to customer rates independent of operating costs.

As a result, the inflow of revenue available for capital cost recovery was virtually leak-free. It was predictable, stable, and conveniently pliant in the face of changing circumstances. Operational exigencies that for other businesses might take money away from capital recovery were met through automatic adjustments to rates that kept returns to shareholders intact. Moreover, the utility and its regulators could make this tightly sealed money pipeline bigger to accommodate the value of a larger base of capital assets. That was also part of the regulatory contract.

The best point in time to begin examining the formation of capital in the electricity sector is after the Second World War. The 1950s and 1960s saw significant acceleration in the demand for electricity, signaling a public interest in capital expansion for electricity infrastructure. Unlike growth during the first half of the 20th Century, however, households were a much larger part of the picture. The number of residential customers increased twice as fast as population growth; more households (and a larger share of the population) became electricity customers. At the same time, industry transitioned from a wartime economy to a consumer economy, in which productivity was becoming more electricity intensive. Consequently, utilities and their regulators saw a robust and sustained growth in electricity demand.

There was some public interest rationale for capital expansion. In 1950, the nation's generation fleet comprised many small plants. Steam-powered plants smaller than 100 MW in nameplate capacity outnumbered larger plants two-to-one. The following decade, however, saw a gradual migration of capital investments to plants that were somewhat larger. One-third of the smaller steam plants were retired by the end of the decade; while during that same time, the number of plants larger than 100 MW more than quadrupled. Better economies of scale created cost savings that could be passed on to customers.

New generator construction kept pace incrementally with growth in demand. Construction work in progress (CWIP), which measures how much a utility has spent during the year on building projects that are not yet finished, remained low throughout most of the 1950s, both in real-dollar terms and in relation to the value of total electric plant in service. Between 1950 and 1968, the value of CWIP for all investor-owned utilities was between 10% and 20% of the net value of generating plant in service. The consistency of CWIP during a period of capacity expansion suggests that the gestation period of new capital—the time between the decision to build a new plant and the time it is placed in service—was relatively short and within a convenient planning horizon for the utility and its regulators.

It was in the 1960s that the nature of electric utility capital investments began to change, not just in volume but in character. These new patterns of investment replaced the previous model of smaller and more modular generators that followed every incremental increase in local demand. The new model was the gigaplant, which formed the basis of the legacy fleet that is with us today.

1960

1970

1980

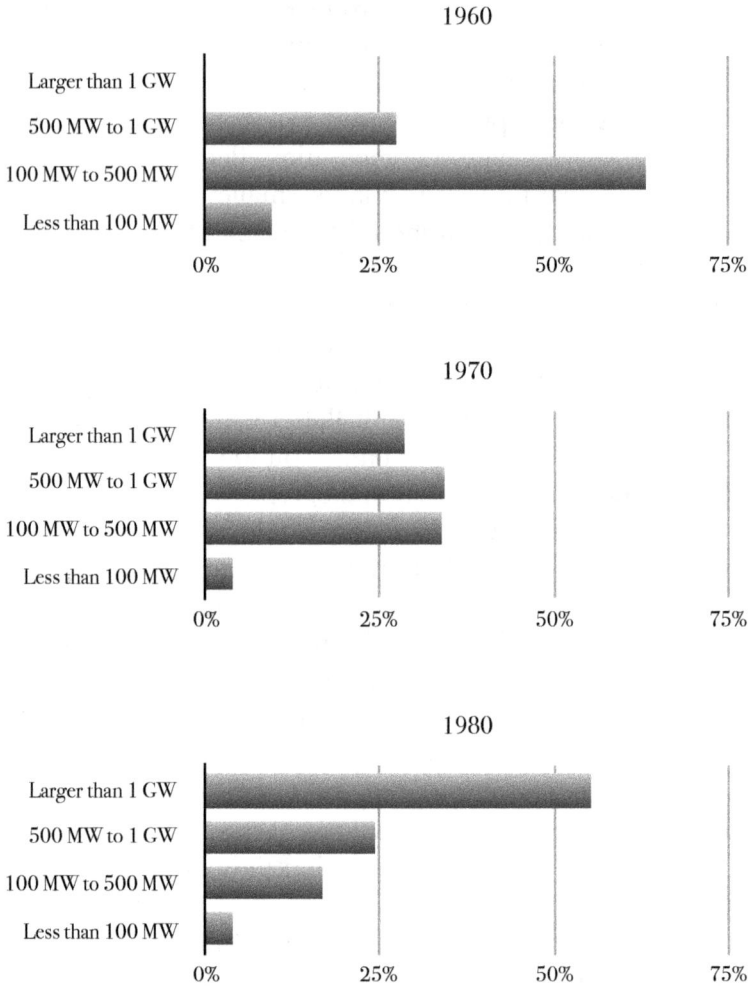

Source: Federal Power Commission, "Statistics of Publicly Owned Electric Utilities in the United States" (various years).

Figure 1: Composition of total U.S. generating capacity, by size of plant

In 1950, about 30% of the nation's steam electric generating capacity was in plants smaller than 100 megawatts; the remaining 70% of total capacity rested with plants larger than 100 megawatts and with an average capacity that was just larger than 220 megawatts. The incremental growth of the 1950s gradually changed the balance. By 1960, plants larger than 100 megawatts outnumbered smaller plants, and their average size increased slightly to 285 megawatts. Plants smaller than 100 megawatts then accounted for just 10% of the nation's total generating capacity.

These numbers are interesting because of how dramatically they changed after 1960. By 1970, the category of small steam plants made up a scant 4% of the nation's steam generating capacity. The bulk was divided about evenly between medium-sized plants (100 megawatts to 500 megawatts), large plants (500 megawatts up to 1 gigawatt), and gigaplants. This shift continued throughout the 1970s so that by 1980 more than half of the nation's steam generating capacity resided in 175 gigaplants.

Unlike generation capacity added in the 1950s, gigaplants required a huge investment of capital and construction took a long time. Consequently, CWIP skyrocketed after 1965. As a percentage of the value of utilities' net generation plant, CWIP ranged from 30% to 60% in the 1970s and reached as high as 70% in 1982.

One attribute of CWIP is that it does not get into customer base rates until the plant is in service. The incremental generation growth of the 1950s and 1960s had largely kept pace with load growth with a relatively short and consistent gestation period for new capital investment. This spread the cost of new generation across a larger pool of customers. The economic result was that inflation-adjusted electricity rates fell steadily. That trend stopped in 1970, when utility customers began picking up the tab for all the new coal gigaplants that were then beginning to come online. Over the next thirteen years, inflation-adjusted

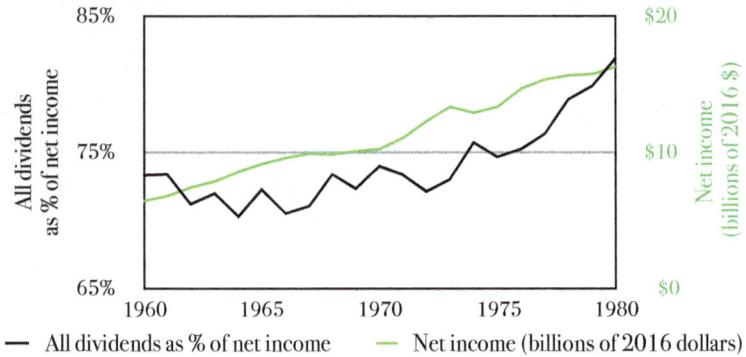

Figure 2: Utility application of net income to dividends

Source: Federal Power Commission, "Statistics of Publicly Owned Electric Utilities in the United States" (various years).

electricity rates stopped falling and instead rose at an average of 2% per year.[32]

The gigaplant model required capital—and a lot of it. Electric utilities did not have a great deal of difficulty attracting it, either. As creditworthy borrowers and equity-issuing businesses, they had an extraordinary advantage over all other capital-seeking businesses: The State's guarantee of minimal risk on returns. No other capital-intensive business enjoyed such protection. Even rising fuel costs were not a serious concern, because these were operational expenses that could be passed through to customers without taking anything away from the dividends paid to shareholders. An upward swing in fuel costs was met by a paral-

---

[32] The Arab oil embargo in 1973-74 and the oil supply disruptions caused by the Iranian revolution in 1979 increased the price of fuel oil and natural gas, but the inflationary effects increased the supply of nearly everything else as well. Inflation during the 1970s was more than four times what it was in the 1960s. Correcting for inflation during this period moderates the impact of the oil crisis considerably.

lel upswing in rates and utility revenues; that was how the regulatory contract worked.

Correcting for inflation, utilities' net income and the value of their generation plant in service both doubled from the beginning of the 1960s to the end of the 1970s. Dividends paid by utilities to shareholders, however, increased at a much faster pace. The share of net earnings paid out in dividends held at a fairly consistent 72% throughout the 1960s but increased to more than 80% by 1980. Dividends paid on preferred stock quadrupled.

Even so, the enormity of the gigaplant investment was still too large for most utilities to swallow on their own, despite their significant improvements in economies of scale. The problem for many utilities was that the scale required to achieve those economies was often larger than their customer bases could reasonably sustain in rates. As a result, many utilities began to enter into joint ventures for shares of a gigaplant. About half of the nation's coal gigaplants and about two thirds of its nuclear gigaplants were jointly owned. Even with joint ownership, however, the capital expansion caused a detectable increase in customer rates as the gigaplants were rolled into the owning utilities' rate bases.

It is worth pointing out that there was little connection between the risks and uncertainties of operating the power system and the investment risk facing banks and shareholders. Gigaplants posed a contingency risk that was not present in the 1950s' collection of smaller generators: What might happen to the rest of the grid if the gigaplant were to come offline quickly and unexpectedly? Compensating for the potential outage of a gigaplant required more backup generation, and occasionally new transmission, to ensure the grid was resilient enough to keep operating without a blackout.

That was not what risk meant to investors, though. For someone holding common stock in a utility, the risk that mattered was whether the utility would earn sufficient net revenue to pay a dividend. How well the gigaplant operated wasn't a serious risk to the investor, so long as the regulatory contract continued to require the utility to collect enough revenue from customers to provide the approved rate of return. In other words, the formation of capital during the era of the gigaplant was not a function of what the gigaplant was capable of doing or how efficiently the utility ran it. Rather, it was a function of how much the plant increased the utility's asset base, coupled with the assurance that revenues would increase enough to provide the same rate of return on the expanded capital base.

The regulatory contract mitigates investment risk in a way not enjoyed by other enterprises seeking to attract capital. It might not be direct cash, but it does significantly enhance the ability to raise capital for investments that otherwise could not be financed. This advantage is exclusive to regulated, monopoly-franchise utilities. The risk-subsidy is provided by the State through the revenue guarantees it provides to the utility: a leak-proof flow of money from a captured customer base in an amount always sufficient to ensure full recovery of capital investments.

Because this protection is predicated on the public interest, the State could have imposed other public interest requirements on how gigaplants were developed. Environmental protection could have been mandated, but many of these gigaplants were conceived, approved, and started before President Richard Nixon and Congress created the Environmental Protection Agency. At the time, scientific knowledge about the effects of sulfur dioxide emissions, nitrogen oxide emissions, mercury, and carbon dioxide emissions was not as extensive as it is today.

Would the additional cost of environmental mitigation have slowed down the gigaplant boom? Such retrospective hypotheticals always risk missing variables obscured by time, but in this case, another thought experiment might be useful. Recall first that costs had little effect on a utility's profitability, because the revenue side was periodically adjusted to keep the utility's overall rate of return consistent. Increasing the cost of an already-large capital investment by insisting on environmental mitigation probably would have been another line item added to CWIP and eventually rolled into rates. More importantly, the additional emission mitigation would likely have increased the value of the asset. From the investors' perspective, this would have been good. With the asset worth more, returns collected from rates would have been bigger. Thus, environmental mitigation probably would not have slowed down gigaplant expansion.

The gigaplants still operating today became financially possible because of the regulatory contract between the State and utilities. Monopoly protection bolstered the financial safety of what would otherwise have been a high-risk capital investment. Instead of a diversified, flexible portfolio of new investment, the regulatory contract encouraged the typical utility to place one large financial bet on a single massive piece of capital. Today these protections are weakening, opening the door for new models of capital formation that will drive what the utility of the future can do.

Merchant Generators

A new model of capital formation for electricity supply began to emerge in the 1990s: merchant generators, or independent power producers. This model has evolved into one of creative destruction's most important vehicles for change. It has accelerated the retirement of much of the old and inefficient stock of capital assets created under the old regulatory contract. Moreover, most of these new power producers have been subject to the rigor of competition and, thus, the expectation that every dollar of invested capital is as productive as possible.

Amendments to the Federal Power Act authorized non-utilities to own and operate generators to provide wholesale power.

These generators did not serve retail customers directly; state laws still governed the utilities' monopoly franchises for serving end-use customers. Merchant generators could, however, sell directly to customer-serving utilities, and later could participate in organized wholesale markets. They could negotiate prices for the power they sold to utilities and other bulk power customers, provided they could demonstrate that they had no market power or any other extraordinary, anti-competitive advantage. (On the buyer's side, deals with regulated utilities were still subject to State approval.)

Merchant generation started slowly. In 1990, these independent power producers provided just 1% of the nation's total generation. However, the advent of organized wholesale power markets at the end of the decade opened up to them a new field of opportunity. By 2000, their share of net generation had increased to 12%; by 2016, it had grown to more than 41%.

In fact, independent power producers—not conventional utilities—made most of the capital investment in new generation capacity between 2000 and 2016, according to data compiled by the U.S. Energy Information Administration. Between 2001 and 2006, most of what these merchant generators added was new natural gas capacity, much of it in the new organized wholesale power markets. From 2007 to 2016, nearly two-thirds was renewable, responding to decreasing costs of wind and solar power as well as increasing demand for clean energy.[33]

Independent producers do not have the magic magnet for capital that the regulatory contract gave utilities. New investment depends on reliable forecasts of fuel and power prices. It also demands project analysis demonstrating within a reasonable

---

[33] Part of the rapid increase in merchant generators' share of the pie was the acquisition of existing assets in strategic markets. The early 2000s saw a flurry of mergers and acquisitions among non-utility generators, and by 2015 the five largest merchant generator parent companies held more than 70% of all combined cycle natural gas generating capacity that had been built prior to 2001.

band of likelihood that market conditions will allow the new generator to operate with enough financial headroom to meet its equity and long-term debt obligations.

But there is no guarantee. The most important difference between independent power producers and utilities is that merchant generators lack the same access to risk protections. By definition, independent power producers only serve wholesale customers and therefore have no direct access to any retail customer revenues—let alone retail revenues that are protected from competition. Merchant generators depend on competitively procured power purchase agreements (PPAs). In organized power markets, they also depend on the prices and dispatch instructions resulting from day-ahead and real-time auctions. Unlike utilities, they have no separately recovered and accounted revenue stream safely earmarked for investors and lenders.

On the other hand, merchant generators have more flexibility in how they structure their capital. Not being under the regulatory contract means capital is not limited geographically to an authorized service territory. The company can seek the best opportunities anywhere, and can combine distant assets into a single portfolio. Equity can come from institutional investors, limited liability corporations, and even utilities that have established merchant generation divisions that operate separately and outside their franchised service territories.

Independent power producers, unlike utilities, are highly sensitive to the volatility of commodity prices. They are thus in the same economic boat as retail customers, despite the lack of any direct commercial relationship between them. High fuel prices increase a merchant generator's operating cost just as they raise the cost of gasoline and home heating for individuals.[34] Utilities, by contrast, do not feel the pinch of operational cost increases directly.

A utility that purchases power from an independent producer has no fiduciary obligation to the merchant generator's investors in this new arrangement. It does still have an obligation to its own retail customers to purchase power at costs that are not much higher than what it would take for the utility to generate the same power itself, however. This defines the market for independent power producers in areas still served by regulated monopoly utilities. Practically, they must be capable of supplying the utility with electricity for less than it would cost the utility to generate the same power from its own stock of resources—a bar made artificially higher by the utility's ability to safely tuck its own investments into rate base.

Thus, the guaranteed flow of money from captured retail customers to capital investments is not a luxury independent power producers enjoy. Money itself needs to be smarter in the merchant generator model. Under the old utility model, where both equity and long-term debt were de-coupled from operational issues by the regulatory contract, investors seldom needed to look beyond the utility's audited financial statement to determine how well the utility was protecting their interests. Bankers did not need to know what a supercritical boiler was or how it worked, because nothing about boiler operations would affect their returns. Today when the investment is a new wind farm, solar facility, or combined cycle plant, it is not as simple. Returns

---

[34] The oil crises of the 1970s, which took a bite out of household incomes, are a prime example. Utility fuel expenses also rose during this time, as many of the newly commissioned gigaplants ran on heavy fuel oil. Fuel costs were largely passed through to customers in the form of rate increases, while revenues for non-fuel expenses were about the same from 1974 to 1980 as they were for the years immediately before the oil embargo. Utility net revenues, which were already increasing as more gigaplants began to add more to utility rate base and were the money pot from which dividends were paid to shareholders, barely registered an impact.

on investment often depend on the characteristics of the site—how windy it is or how close to available transmission. Revenues for a new combined cycle plant will depend on how much unused capacity there is on existing plants in the market and on whether the new plant operates at a constant level or whether it follows demand up in the morning and down in the evening.

The relevance of such details with respect to an investment caused a change in the business culture of lenders in the early years of the wind power boom. Equity partners and bankers were often caught by surprise when transmission congestion limited the production—and consequently the revenues—of early wind projects. From 2001 through 2003, for example, nearly all wind development in West Texas occurred near existing transmission in an area with reasonably good wind resources. While each project by itself looked good on paper, the aggregate development overwhelmed the local grid to the point that system operators had to issue curtailment orders routinely, which in turn reduced the wind developers' revenues across the board. Today, equity partners and lenders ask more sophisticated questions about transmission access and other operational factors that could affect the return on their investments—something that earlier investors did not need to do with respect to new giga-plants.

The merchant generator model puts more demand on capital to produce than the regulatory contract ever did. But it also creates less certainty that an individual investment will do so. If the market is providing correct price signals (which is critical), the return on investment is tied to the amount of economic benefit the investment provides to society. Capital is squandered otherwise. Most crucial: the project's investors, not the public, bear the loss if the project fails. Attracting capital in the first place often depends on proving to investors that the project is good enough and the conditions ripe enough to provide a reasonable expectation of profit in the face of the market's inherent uncertainty.

Today the largest merchant generators, like the utility holding companies of the early 20th Century, have diversified holdings in many different markets with as many as four or five corporate tiers. But the comparison with conventional utilities largely stops there, because whether their assets produce a return on equity depends on how competitive they are in the markets where they operate. Efficiency matters, and business mistakes cannot be swept under the rug of a captured customer base. Independent power producers feel the economic tempests of volatile fuel prices—not to mention volatile wholesale power prices—far more than the traditional electric utility. Basically, merchant generators live and struggle in the same type of economic environment as nearly everyone else.

Price Signals, Part 1

In this new world, price signals must be right. This could be the most important economic principle for decision makers to understand as they rethink the public interest in the electric sector. The signals need to be linked to behaviors that, at the end of the day, lead to a reduction in the social cost of providing electricity.[35] The prices that inform an economic decision must therefore arise from factors that accurately capture how the decision might affect the whole market.

This brings us to one of the most important characteristics of the future utility: Capital formation ceases to be the centralized command-and-control social decision it used to be. Instead,

---

[35] Even end-use customers will find themselves more exposed to the economic karma of cost-causation in the electricity sector's new world. Their decisions and behaviors, too, can cost or save money. Some customers cost more to serve than others, and this has always been true. What is changing is the great normalization that occurred in the rates customers were charged, which tended to make customers economically indifferent to the cost consequences of different behaviors. I will return to this in Chapter 5.

it becomes a series of decisions made by individuals operating in a fog of market uncertainty. Rate case intervenors do not have a chance to weigh in on whether they think an investment is prudent. Each investment is a private business decision made by individual market participants and their lenders. The decision is based on whether the project has a reasonable chance of providing its investors with a rate of return that is comparable to (if not better than) what they could earn investing their money elsewhere.

This shift in how investment decisions are made is ground-zero of creative destruction. The business environment itself must provide individual market participants with the right economic signals for all types of decisions. Prices and all other risk signals precipitating from the chaos of market activity must accurately reflect conditions of supply and demand. The causal links between market conditions and price signals must be valid and cannot be distorted either by deliberate manipulation or poorly considered rules with unintended consequences. Impersonal market conditions transcend any individual market participant, and yet they are crucial to reaching outcomes that are economically efficient and socially beneficial.

That is not how utilities and regulators of the past were acculturated. Their world was driven by socially made investment decisions that were definitive and financially safe (with respect to cost recovery), but not necessarily efficient. Going from that to a world where investment decisions have only an individual investor's field of vision requires a psychological change. Triggers for new investment become responses to immediately observable conditions—such as price signals.

The most important thing prices signal is when to invest in a new power plant. Traditional utilities did not look to market prices for that signal. They looked at the system reserve margin: the difference between peak demand and the amount of generating capacity physically available to meet that demand.[36] One strength of the old regulatory contract model was that if load growth trends pointed toward diminished reserve margins ten years out, the utility could get approval to start adding the capacity well in advance of the need. When load forecasts projected that the reserve margin was falling below the critical threshold, the word would move up through the utility to executive planners. These planners would then initiate a regulatory request to build new generation capacity and put it into the rate base. Economic efficiency barely came into play.

The downside was that the market provided no restraining counterbalance if the utility wanted to overbuild. Each decision to add new capacity was an administrative exercise that ended with approval or rejection by the State. The final decision by the regulator could be influenced by a host of non-monetary factors such as outside political influence, the regulators' own experience and expertise, and public opposition. If the utility could convince its regulator that the plant was a prudent investment—even if the reserve margin showed no indication of contracting any time soon—the regulatory contract would provide capital protection.

Outside the regulatory contract, a diminishing reserve margin indicates a scarcity condition that (in theory) results in higher prices, provided that market prices move with alacrity in response to supply and demand. These pricing signals should be the cue for generation owners to invest in new capacity. But there can be complications. Scarcity of generation is not all that can push power prices higher. Power prices are also a function of the price of fuel used to generate power. This means that wholesale power prices can rise or fall driven by factors other than a

---

[36] Utilities will typically use some threshold value for the size of the margin (usually, available generation capacity that is 10% to 20% greater than the maximum demand during the year). When reserves fall below the critical threshold, the system faces a risk of reliability problems that could even result in blackouts.

shrinking margin between supply and demand. Another compli- cation is that as prices more closely track supply and demand conditions, they differentiate by location and by the type of re- source required. Scarcity can be local within an area with limited transmission infrastructure. Some special types of resources, such as generators that can ramp up or down quickly to follow real-time variations in demand, can be scarce even when there is an abundance of older but slower capacity.

Moreover, even if high power prices reflect legitimate scarci- ty of supply, they naturally tend to retreat once new capacity is brought on line. Thus, producers and their lenders need to base investment decisions not on current prices, but on what they ex- pect prices to be once the market reaches equilibrium with the new supply.[37]

The question, then, is whether post-investment market prices will provide enough revenue for a new generator to justify in- vestment in the project. If they do not—or more to the point, if market conditions signal that they will not—then new capital will go elsewhere until things change.

The U.S. electricity sector began to bifurcate between tradi- tional utilities and organized wholesale markets in the late 1990s. The new markets were operated by what eventually came to be known as regional transmission organizations (RTOs) and repre- sented a major change in grid operations. They separated the business of owning and managing the transmission system from the business of owning and operating electric generators. RTOs offered merchant generators more opportunities, especially if the

---

[37] Renewables (particularly wind power after 2000) added another market wrinkle. An increasing amount of generation with zero marginal cost tends to drive down the price of power. While this lowers costs for retail customers, it can also affect the potential cash flow of an investment new conventional generation even when physical scarcity conditions arise. Competitive whole- sale markets include safeguard mechanisms designed to compensate for low energy prices that might occur under scarcity conditions.

generator operated more efficiently than legacy units built by the utilities.

Prices in an RTO market respond quickly to supply and demand conditions but can be volatile. This raised concerns that price volatility would make investment too uncertain to finance a new generator. Market auctions for setting energy prices were usually adequate for the recovery of fuel costs and other variable operating costs, but prices need to provide enough revenue above that to cover the new generator's capital costs. If they do not, new investment won't happen even when the reserve margin diminishes. This came to be known as a "missing money" dilemma.

RTOs have developed two models for incentivizing new capacity. Both rely on price signals—additional money extracted from load to augment revenues from market energy prices and designed to make new generation a good investment when shortages begin to appear. Both are also nondiscriminatory, in that they do not administratively choose who gets to build new generation capacity. This is different from the old utility model, where regulators picked which new generator should be included in rates paid by end-use customers. The market-wide price signals are intended to become more intense as the metrics for systemwide shortage increase, receding once market participants respond by bringing new capacity onto the market.

The two approaches differ in how the payments are extracted from the market. They also create different political risks for regulators providing market oversight.

One approach is an energy-only market, which relies on market energy prices to signal persistent supply shortage and the need for new capacity. Market rules do not limit how high prices can rise (or if there are price caps, they are very high). While price manipulation is a risk, the presumption embedded in market design is that a high energy price indicates legitimate supply scarcity. It assumes high prices are not being caused by an entity whose share of the market is large enough to give it market power. Abundant supply will depress prices; scarcity will drive prices higher; new generators will be operationally more efficient than old generators; and a balanced market will produce prices that tend to be high enough for a new generator to have net revenues large enough to pay its capital costs.

The other approach is a forward capacity market. When the system reserve margin approaches a threshold level, the RTO creates a supplemental payment to generators intended to bolster the ability to recover capital costs. The payment level is set by an auction process that identifies the minimum price that generators will accept.[38] One important feature of these capacity payments is that they do not depend on how often the new generator is dispatched for providing energy or on the prices that prevail in the energy market. Consequently, a forward capacity market will often be coincident with market rules limiting the offer prices generators may submit into the energy market.

An energy-only market is not for the politically faint of heart. Price spikes that are thousands of dollars per megawatt-hour make for scary headlines, even if they only occur for a few minutes. Politicians once fervent in their support for markets when the balance between supply and demand was placidly abundant can change their tune once constituents start voicing their fears about high prices.

But forward capacity markets come with their own political difficulties. At first blush, the mechanism looks and smells like welfare for generation owners: They get money without having to generate any electricity. Never mind that the alternatives are wild price spikes and shortage-induced blackouts. If understanding how the mechanism works takes an advanced degree in eco-

---

[38] Capacity markets also allow load participation. If a large consumer can prove systematic energy efficiency and a permanent reduction in demand, the customer may participate in the auction at a certain price and, if accepted, can earn the capacity payment.

nomics or systems theory, to most people it may look like a black box controlling a large amount of customer money. That will naturally draw suspicion from those who are not power sector professionals themselves.

Neither of these "missing money" solutions is perfect, and both continue to evolve as the easy questions give way to more complicated ones. What is important is the evolution's direction and what it means for capital formation. Both solutions aim to augment market prices in a way that does not distort the investment signals. In both cases the past insulation from risk is gone. Attracting new capital is linked more rigorously (and more unforgivingly) to the real economic good the investment provides to society. More than anything else, this complex economic and political equation is the reason technology alone is not the key to understanding the utility of the future.

Re-linking Capital Formation and Efficiency

Creative destruction's hammer blow to the gigaplant model is that capital loses its protection from the consequences of operational inefficiency. To an ever-increasing extent, poor performance in the utility of the future risks failing to recover the cost of capital investment. Returns on equity are hardwired to the economic benefits that a new capital investment provides to society in a way they were not under the regulatory contract. Investors risk more when actual benefits fall short of conceptual benefits, and this imposes a new constraint on the amount of capital the market is willing to place on a single investment.

Yet only in the old world of traditional electric utilities is this unusual or even noteworthy. Anywhere else in the capitalist economy, the balance between risk and return is a normal defining characteristic of any investment. Institutional investors always pay attention to a company's credit rating, management history, net income trends, and other metrics that show the company's record for putting capital to productive use.

Re-linking capital formation and productivity will tend to slow down the scalability of new investment. Super-sizing a generation project will no longer be as financially feasible as it was in the 1960s and 1970s when the regulatory contract shielded such investments from risk. Institutional investors will more frequently insist on asset diversity, pushing new capital investments away from a few very large assets and towards many smaller assets.

Efficient operations are crucial both to capital cost recovery and to the overall productivity of capital. The value of a capital investment is reflected in the price it fetches for what it produces. When per-unit prices are market-driven, an individual producer's competitiveness will depend on keeping per-unit production costs below the per-unit prices in the wider market. The gap between per-unit prices and the generator's per-unit cost of production is what determines the producer's ability to attract new capital: The lower the producer's cost, the bigger its margin, and the more returns it can offer on equity.

The productive efficiency of capital is therefore more crucial than ever. We may think of the productivity of capital as the amount of economic good provided by each dollar of invested capital. Consider two projects each having a capital cost of $1 billion. If one project delivers 50% more electricity to customers than the other, it will have the greater productivity of capital. Because each dollar of capital investment is producing more benefit, it is earning more total revenue from which capital costs can be repaid. Greater capital productivity also frees up capital for investment elsewhere in the economy.

Poor productivity of capital is ultimately an economic albatross hanging from society's neck. Its effects ripple throughout the economy in the form of

- *less disposable income,* with consumers paying more for electricity service and thereby having less spending power for other things;

85

- *lower real wages* (wages and productivity are linked, and underperforming capital and technology can make labor less productive); and
- *less tax revenue for social services*, such as schools and roads.

A few states with renewable energy targets (California, most notably) have chosen to bear this deadweight. These states deliberately discourage the use of wind and solar resources developed in neighboring states where the productivity of capital—megawatt-hours delivered for every dollar of investment—is higher than in their own. While the political rationale is often the purported protection of in-state jobs, the full range of economic consequences can more than offset the permanent jobs that might be created. Advanced generation is capital intensive and technology intensive, not labor intensive.

Any electric sector investment needs to pass two tests of merit. The first is whether it adds economic value to society at large. This can be through reducing the cost of creating a social good (in this case, the delivery of electricity to retail customers), or through avoiding harm or loss in a more cost-effective manner (avoiding regional blackouts or service disruptions, for example). It can also be an investment that creates a new type of social good or adds to an existing social good, as happens when renewable energy replaces coal-fueled generation and thereby reduces pollution in addition to providing electricity.

The second, and equally important, test is whether it provides a return on investment. To understand what this means, consider new distribution technologies such as smart metering. The technical possibilities for greater reliability and reduced cost are tremendous, but the savings depend on how customers change their behavior. If the utility relies solely on smart grid technology's "wow" factor as a reason for customers to install smart thermostats, smart lighting controls, and more sophisticated demand-side management devices, the response will most likely be anemic. The investment needs to include an avenue for the participating customer to share in the benefits—not in an indirect and general way through lower base rates, but directly by being paid for the changes in behavior that underlie the broader benefits. Broader economically driven participation makes for a more robust revenue flow, one that is more likely to provide a predictable return on the investment.

One hallmark of creative destruction is the bursting forth of new value sources that erode the economic foundations of old technologies. But unless the flow of new value reaches all the way to providing a reliable return on new investment, the promise of new technology will go no further than a handful of demonstration projects that have little real transformational effect on the sector.

One might ask: If inefficient capital is such a problem now, why wasn't it before? One reason is that the thermal generation technologies that made up much of the investment under the regulatory contract were labor intensive. Productivity was not just a matter of capital; it was also a matter of having enough of a labor force to move coal and procure natural gas supplies. Another reason is that capital efficiency did not matter in a financially tangible way. Once the State approved a new project for inclusion in the utility's rate base, capital cost recovery was guaranteed. How efficiently the investment was used had no effect on capital cost recovery.

There will be a period of time in a transitioning market when risk-protected capital will be competing head-to-head with new investments that do not enjoy comparable protection. If the field is not level, competitive merit can be suppressed to the unfair disadvantage of an efficiently managed capital investment. The new cadre of competitive developers and risk-aware investors can do all the right things yet still not be able to earn a return on capital. This highlights an important role for the State: Smoothing the transition to the new paradigm will very likely require some temporary measures to prevent the old world from standing in the way of the new. Legacy generation (as well as the layout of the bulk transmission system serving it) has a built-in anticompetitive advantage over newcomers. State action can curb this advantage until it ceases to distort price signals in the matured competitive environment.

The Growing Role of Entrepreneurs

Among the most important economic functionaries in the new electricity sector are entrepreneurs. They have been peripheral to the electric sector for at least half a century, but that is changing. As the next two chapters will explain in more detail, many of the opportunities likely to arise in this new economic paradigm are outside the organizational sphere of the corporate entities that have functioned as electric utilities. Detecting and releasing the unconventional pockets of value takes the skill sets of an entrepreneur.

As a corporation with a regulated public function, the traditional utility operated through established norms and repeatable patterns of activity. This milquetoast predictability can be traced back to the regulatory contract. The monopoly, having few competitive checks and balances on the cost effectiveness of its operation, was obliged to account for how it used every dollar of revenue towards the generation and delivery of electricity whenever it came before its regulators with a request to change rates. Any innovation that represented a deviation from the established patterns had to be justified for its financial prudence to ensure that no money collected from the public through rates would be wasted. That favored practices certain to produce results, and it discouraged any innovation when the benefits were uncertain.

While the public interest was limited to low cost and high reliability, the utility's appetite for innovation was modest. As the public interest expands, new technologies require new decision-making tools and decision protocols. This demands innovation to an extent new to utilities, and that conflicts in many ways with corporate cultures that have had decades to solidify.

The entrepreneur's function in the economy is very different organizationally and culturally. Being outside the corporate space of the utility, the entrepreneur has no regulatory contract influencing decisions—no burden of regulatory micro-accounting, but no financial protection either. Risk is a natural part of what the entrepreneur does, and the only arbiter of whether a risk pays off is whether it succeeds in the market. If it fails, the entrepreneur (and any financial backers) suffer the loss entirely. If it succeeds, the profits to the entrepreneur are limited only by what the market will bear. As Schumpeter points out:

> To undertake such new things is difficult and constitutes a distinct economic function, first, because they lie outside of the routine tasks which everybody understands and, secondly, because the environment resists in many ways that vary, according to social conditions, from simple refusal either to finance or to buy a new thing, to physical attack on the man who tries to produce it.[39]

Resistance intensifies as a new undertaking moves from niche to mainstream, and it becomes evident that an old ox is about to be gored. Renewable energy, for example, faced little outright opposition when its application barely extended beyond solar panels on space missions. When large-scale wind power reached commercial takeoff, however, enemies appeared. Especially in organized markets, such as Texas, a larger amount of wind power in the system had the effect of reducing prices, reducing the revenues of thermal generators. This engendered political opposition by some thermal generation interests against any policies enabling further renewable energy expansion.

---

[39] Schumpeter, *Capitalism, Socialism, and Democracy* (*supra* at note 27).

The retail side also has entrepreneurial opportunities. One challenge entrepreneurs will likely face here is the tension between the demand for more choice and the desire for simplicity. These two forces work in opposite directions, and reconciling them in the most efficient and profitable manner requires the skill set of an entrepreneur. Energy management consultants currently help large commercial and industrial customers reduce their energy costs through monitoring consumption, improving process efficiency, and taking advantage of different energy pricing plans. This role could expand to small businesses and groups of residential customers if the reforms discussed in the next two chapters result in tangible price signals. But it does require customers to think harder about how they use electricity; and while most profit-driven businesses are willing to do that, many individuals place a premium on convenience. The entrepreneur's challenge is to figure out how to reduce complexity for individuals so that more are willing to change, while maintaining the value and profitability of providing an innovative, useful service.

In his general economic framework, Schumpeter portrayed the relationship between corporate capitalists and independent entrepreneurs as organizationally cannibalistic. To the extent that the corporation was driven to a need for innovation (by competition, consumer demand, or the need to protect the economic viability of its existing capital investments), management would tend to absorb the entrepreneurial ventures it required into its own organization. Capitalism would systematize innovation as a new factor of production. Some utilities have certainly taken such a path by, for example, establishing affiliated unregulated merchant generation companies that compete in markets outside the regulated utility's service territory.

Schumpeter drew the pessimistic conclusion that capitalism's consumption of entrepreneurs would be one of the factors contributing to its downfall. I would argue, however, that the electricity sector will follow a different path, one that is in fact more

90

adaptive than Schumpeter foresaw. Capital formation for the utility of the future is more disaggregated and more agile. Instead of billions of dollars sunk into one massive gigaplant, many smaller bundles of investments are distributed across a diverse array of opportunities. The success of capital investments depends more closely on real economic value. Translating price signals into value involves information-intensive operation and new ways to systematize that information. This all adds up to a need for innovation and alacrity that have been outside the culture of traditional utilities.

Naturally, some investment ventures will be speculative. Innovation may be varied and will naturally be hit-or-miss. Recall a point raised in the previous chapter. The new public interest does not lie in making everyone adopt a new way of doing things. Rather, it lies in giving individuals the freedom to adopt new ways of doing things—if they are willing to take the responsibilities and risks on themselves.

Whether this adds up to customers bearing more or less of the weight of capital costs is difficult to predict. Two countervailing influences are at work. On one hand, the direct cost of borrowing will tend to be higher because the risk protection once given by the regulatory contract will be gone: More risk generally demands higher returns. On the other hand, society (as it used to be embodied in a utility's captured customer base) will not have to absorb the cost of failure.

One important public interest decision the State must make is whether to attempt to get utilities to act more like entrepreneurs, or to change the utilities' function so that they can provide a platform for entrepreneurial innovation. The next chapter will develop the concept of *market maker*, which I've introduced and briefly touched on earlier in this book. If the public interest acknowledges the weakening of natural monopoly in some parts of the supply chain and re-orients utilities towards those specific functions that are still natural monopolies, it will set the stage for a new type of relationship between the entrepreneur and the utility. The entrepreneur with a potentially profitable business model will neither compete with the utility nor be assimilated by it. Instead, the independent venture will stay independent and will be eligible to compete with other independent ventures in the same market. The utility's role as market maker would be to manage the information interfaces between the independent competitors and the rest of the grid's operation.

Creative Destruction and the Utility of the Future

The formation of capital for the utility of the past was a peculiar function of the public interest and how it was expressed through the regulatory contract. Without this institutional element, the legacy gigaplants we have today could not have happened. Even so, it was never sustainable. Load growth is no longer driving investment in new generating plants. Monopoly is no longer a binding feature of the utility landscape. On top of that, the peculiar features of the public interest for which electric utilities were custodians are evolving.

In short, the gigaplant model is done.

Creative destruction in the electric sector is affecting capital formation in several significant and related ways. First, the economic protection afforded to utilities by the State under the regulatory contract is giving way to a tougher and more demanding financial regimen. Risk is real. The revenue stream needed to meet debt service and other capital requirements is in many cases no longer guaranteed. More capital investments by utilities are subject to closer and more careful assessments of risk, similar to capital enterprises that do not have the safety of a regulatory contract. Overall, the sources of capital are demanding more homework from proponents of new projects.

Being forced into a risk-sensitive capital pool is causing another change in the electric sector: Big is out; small is in. Large generators that require committing large amounts of capital are more difficult to justify. Rather than putting so many chips on one high-risk bet, investors are looking for diversification. Much of the new capacity coming online is smaller, and portfolios are diverse technologically and even geographically. The market's appetite for new large generating stations is small.

The movement toward leanness and efficiency also means capital will look for portfolio quality. Being one of many will not by itself be enough. The ideal resource portfolio functions as a synergistic whole, comprising investments that are compatible and complementary. This replaces the approach of classifying a new unit as base load, intermediate resource, or peaker and then operating each separately within the profile. Valuable attributes of each capital asset will be its ability to interface with information management systems, its ability to respond flexibly to instructions communicated through the information management system, and its ability to support renewables and other different resources in the portfolio. Capital formation will increasingly be in the context of an operating portfolio.

The realities of the new utility sector place another demand on capital formation: Investments must be able to play with commodity volatility instead of being threatened by it. This means an increasing ability to respond to price signals up and down the supply chain. Many rate structures currently in place cannot provide these price signals, and this will put new and challenging demands on utility regulators.

Finally, capital formation for the utility of the future will not be predicated on one commercial entity providing all aspects of electric service. Here, the implication is that new investment will anticipate some business interface between the utility and entrepreneurs outside the utility's chain of command. While this may appear to introduce management risk, it actually expands growth opportunities. The utility will still be centrally positioned with respect to operating the transmission system, for example. Other functions (customer load management, for example) will demand more entrepreneurial agility. Dividing the investment stream allows capital to flow to enterprises that are best suited to a particular activity.

All this is key to understanding what the utility of the future can and cannot do, yet it is often overlooked. Already there have been cases where the introduction of new and supposedly "disruptive" technology has failed because of insufficient consideration of how the economic environment has changed. At its most fundamental level, creative destruction is not about new technological gadgets. It is about new ways of creating and using capital.

Chapter 4: Fragmentation

Creative destruction is causing deep fissures in the old electric utility monolith, calling into question the foundational premise of the regulatory contract. Protecting society against monopoly abuses becomes less of a public interest imperative when the monopoly itself is crumbling of natural economic causes. The cracks run vertically and horizontally, spawning new opportunities and challenging old inefficiencies that benefitted once-protected interests.

Fragmentation is a fundamental feature of the utility of the future, but the narrative is not as simple as economic theory might make it appear. There is still a public interest that constrains the economic logic. Whether fragmentation leads to an electricity sector that increases social welfare depends on economic preconditions that vary from one region to the next, and in some places might not yet exist at all. Managing these new factors creates the need for a new type of entity: the *market maker*. These two matters—the heterogeneity of change and the role of the market maker—are crucial to how creative destruction and the public interest intersect.

The ability to move and manage large amounts of information has made fragmentation possible. That is not *why* fragmentation is occurring, however. The force driving creative destruction and its resulting fragmentation is the evolving collective economic consciousness of society with respect to electricity. This is not just a simple matter of new technology. Demands for personal and commercial fulfillment are becoming more informed, and in turn expectations are becoming more diverse. This economic evolution is bringing society's relationships with the electric sector to a crossroads. The well-worn path is the way of the integrated utility regulated by the State. The new path is the way of the fragmented utility sector, with new regulatory requirements. The choice: Which path best gets society to economic outcomes consistent with today's desires and new expectations?

The market restructuring that has taken place in parts of the United States and other parts of the world is the first big step toward the more fragmented utility of the future. Restructuring unbundles the electric sector's major components and infuses them with competition where conditions can support it. This process tends to fragment the electric sector into its four supply chain components.

- *Generation*: The hardware that converts kinetic or other types of energy into electricity
- *Transmission*: The network of high-voltage wires that links the points where bulk electricity is generated with the drop-off points where electricity is routed to end users
- *Distribution*: The network of lower voltage wires that deliver electricity from a drop-off point on the bulk energy system to each individual end user
- *Retail service*: The business arrangement between an end-use customer and a provider for the delivery of electricity; the point where electricity is sold to the customer

In the classic model of vertically-integrated monopoly utilities, these are four *functions* that the electric utility performed itself and coordinated within its own internal operations. In the utility of the future, these are four different segments of independent businesses. Each segment and each business within a segment contributes to a market-guided supply chain in much the same way that farmers, processors, truckers, and grocery stores are all independently-owned enterprises involved in getting food from the field to the dinner table.

The information needed to keep the four components in operational balance is massive and complex. Unlike commodities like wheat, crude oil, and tennis shoes, the commodity produced by the bulk energy system—electrons—cannot be readily stock-piled for later use. This means that the electricity each generator produces *now* must be used *now* somewhere on the bulk energy system. Doing so involves monitoring demand and issuing in-structions for thousands of points on the grid simultaneously and instantaneously. In the most advanced markets, "instantaneous" means every five minutes—not a job an operator can do in vol-ume simply by picking up the phone.

Greater informational complexity might seem like it should require more control and organizational consolidation. In prac-tice, however, the informational requirements have enabled something new: automated, quantitative optimization of grid operations. Complexity requires *coordination* among diverse economic actors. Coordination, however, does not require the control of all assets under consolidated ownership. Several own-ers may have several assets in different segments of the bulk en-ergy system. If all the assets are subject to the same operating criteria, this is no different from having all assets owned by the utility.

Creative destruction is driving change in two spheres of competition: wholesale and retail. Competition in the wholesale market encompasses the creation of electricity by many produc-ers; competition in the retail market involves many providers de-livering electricity service to end-use customers. Profit in either sphere depends on keeping costs below revenues and on manag-ing risk. These, in turn, depend on the efficient flow of opera-tional information and the integrity of price signals. Competi-tion is the first attribute of sectoral fragmentation, and the first thing one needs to understand about the electricity sector's transformation.

The Market Maker

As creative destruction shakes apart the public interest foun-dations of the old utility paradigm, different utility functions are

	MARKET MAKER	
COMPETING POWER GENERATORS	• *Operate day-ahead and real-time wholesale markets for unit dispatch, prices* • *Conduct financial settlement to pay generators for electricity provided, charge retailers for electricity taken* • *Provide retailers with customer meter data* • *Implement common information protocols for all market participants* • *Remain revenue neutral; no stake in any market outcome*	COMPETING RETAIL PROVIDERS

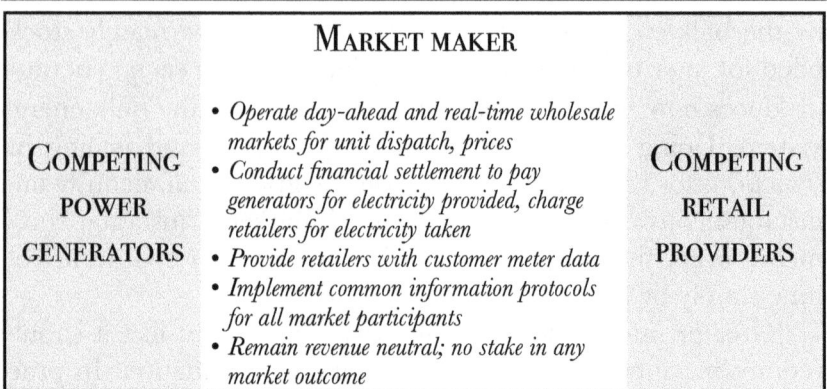

Figure 3: Role of the market maker

emerging; while traditional functions, like generation and providing retail service, become competitive non-utility activities. Market maker is a new *utility* function, one that is essential to the public interest.

The utility as market maker interacts with all the non-utility entities that are competing to do things that old-world utilities used to do. This new function is a natural monopoly, in that two parallel market makers cannot serve the same market without causing confusion. The public interest that these market makers serve is to enable fair competition among the new non-utility players engaged in the generation of electricity and the provision of retail service to end-use customers.

Physically operating the grid involves a multitude of decisions that must be coordinated over time. The role of the market maker is to be a bridge between the rapid-fire operational decisions needed to keep the lights on and the commercial decisions made by individual businesses competing in the market. The market maker manages information—impartially so that competition is fair and efficiently so that the grid does not descend into chaos and blackout.

Market makers have already emerged in the world's organized wholesale markets. They started as independent system operators, expanding into the role of regional transmission organization (RTO). Organized wholesale power markets operated by RTOs are each governed by open rules of operation that are equally applicable to all market competitors. Among the functions that these market makers perform are:

- Providing a common platform for submitting offers and bids into real-time and day-ahead energy markets
- Running the dispatch algorithms that determine which of the market's many independent power producers will run during any given operating period at the least cost, based on the offers and bids submitted
- Reporting the prices that come out of each iteration of the market
- Conducting financial settlement for generation-owing entities, load-serving entities, and all other wholesale market participants.

At the retail level, the market maker ensures the integrity of customer usage data, so that any retail service provider chosen by the customer can provide and bill the services the customer has demanded. It provides and maintains the distribution lines that serve the neighborhood. It combines information about all the retail activity on the distribution grid, feeding the aggregated data smoothly into the activities of the market maker for wholesale activities.

The distribution function retains some of the most compelling arguments for maintaining a utility's monopoly protection. Many of the reasons for this are the same as those that justified monopolies at the beginning of the electricity sector's commercial existence in the late 19th Century. A utility's generators were located near the customers they served, and were linked with a tight network of distribution lines. The need for easements across public and private property made regulated monopoly the only reasonable way to reconcile the public convenience of having electricity service and the public inconvenience of the associated wires and generators. These same public interest issues—minimizing the intrusion of infrastructure on private property and maintaining local reliability—are still relevant to the utility of the future.

In markets that have travelled the furthest down the road of restructuring, the distribution functions of the old vertically integrated utilities have transformed into independent distribution-only utilities. They continue to be regulated, with the wholesale generation of electricity and the packaging of retail service severed from the utility and open to competition.

Market maker—either wholesale or retail—is a role that has no natural place anywhere in the old utility paradigm. A vertically integrated utility generated power and delivered it to end-use customers; a market maker does neither. A government regulator exercised rate making authority, approved or rejected capital investments for rate recovery, and set standards and boundaries for how the integrated utility dealt with its customers. A market maker has no authority to do any of these things. Like an engineer on a train, the market maker's task is to get the entire machine to its destination by ensuring everything runs smoothly and efficiently. It doesn't decide who gets to ride or where they disembark, and it doesn't set fares.

Vertically integrated utilities had no market maker function because they were not a market. More to the point, all the information that the utility needed to make real-time operational decisions was possessed by the utility internally. Coordination was always just a phone call away to someone in another department. When these decisions shift from a monolithic utility to a competitive market comprising hundreds of independent participants, there is no longer any built-in coordination among all points where decisions are made. Yet the information is just as necessary to each decision as it ever was. Managing all this information in an impartial manner requires a bundle of skills, values, protocols, interventions, and decisions unlike anything naturally possessed by any entity coming from the old world of regulated utilities.

A market maker's unique characteristics lie not only in its technical capabilities, however, but also in its relationship to market participants, government authorities, and anyone affected by market outcomes. Market participants need to trust the market, and for that to happen, the market maker needs to be perceived as a fair agent. The market maker must be:

Nondiscriminatory. All market participants are treated the same. A market participant's actions in the market, not its ownership, are what govern market outcomes for the participant.

Disinterested. The market maker cannot itself offer competitive services, nor should it have any ownership ties with any competitive market participant. Even a perception of a potential conflict of interest can undermine confidence in the market.

Non-arbitrary. Actions taken by the market maker to sustain the operation of the market must be based on clear decision rules and formulas. Any market participant affected by a decision should be able to trace the conditions that led to any outcome.

Transparent. The processes by which operating protocols and standards are developed must be open to representatives of all affected stakeholder groups.

Subject to oversight. The market maker cannot be the ultimate judge of its own decisions. Its role is ministerial.

As the previous two chapters explained, commercial relationships in the future utility space are less forgiving of inefficiency and bad business decisions, because there is no longer a publicly-funded regulatory rug under which to sweep the consequences. Risk management is far more important than was the case for traditional utilities, which is one reason impartial and efficient management of information is extremely important. If an old-world utility made a decision that at the time seemed prudent but turned out wrong, the regulatory contract condoned passing the cost of the mistake on to the utility's captured customer base. In the utility of the future, with more decisions and more risk on the shoulders of non-utility competitors, the consequences of error fall to the company that made the mistake, not to society. Without the backstop provided by the regulatory contract, effective risk management is more important that it was for the old-world utility. Full information is key to rationalizing the risk present in the market.

One important reason the market maker has to function as a monopoly utility is the protection of proprietary or confidential information that is essential to operating the market. The line between information that is legitimately confidential and information that should be available is often fuzzy, however. Along this fuzzy line, jockeying among market participants to keep information hidden can be fierce. Thus, one additional role of the market maker—a role that can require intervention by the State for ultimate arbitration—is to publish and implement common rules of transparency that divide confidential information from public information in a manner equally applicable to all market participants.

Competition

When monopoly is no longer natural, competition strives to become the new "natural." This is one of the most important qualities of the new paradigm for arbitrating economic choices in the new and ever-more-fragmented electricity sector. Decision-making through competition is different from how decisions are made by old-world utilities operating under the protection of the regulatory contract. It is less forgiving of inefficiency and mistakes and stingy in its willingness to grant out-of-market preferences. It may react badly if political forces attempt to protect a favored operation from the consequences of economic evolution.

Human nature drives competition. Therefore, it is important to understand with great clarity and depth what human impulses are at work. Competition is a condition of the entire commercial sphere, but it is fundamentally the aggregation of many individuals' impulses. These individuals differ in resources, aptitude, luck, market insight, and how they balance social and ethical values.

Each market participant is driven by a desire to maximize its own individual well-being, according to how well-being is understood by that person or entity. Well-being may be entirely based on immediate monetary profit, or it may be a strategic stream of benefit that foregoes short-term profit in exchange for long-term viability or less risk. Alternatively, it may place value on public visibility that enhances social goals, such as establishing a reputation for improving the environment.

The assumption of neoclassical economics that each market actor is a "profit maximizer" is therefore useful only if it is broadly construed to include things besides immediate monetary gain. Thus, the field of competition comprises individual actors, each seeking to maximize its profit, where "profit" is understood as a highly diverse matrix of goals.

Broadly speaking, competition can be divided into two categories—competition to profit from creating new economic value and competition to secure economic rents. Distinguishing between these two competitive drivers is important for the future utility, because rent-seeking can suffocate the creation of value if not managed sensibly. (Recall from Chapter 2 the unbridled rent-seeking by utility holding companies in the 1920s and its consequences on the overall economy.) This would undermine the public interest value of competition.

The conventional arena for competition is in the creation of new economic value. This takes the form of providing goods or services at a lower price or in a manner that better suits the customer's preferences. Such competition is formalized in organized wholesale power markets through the use of auctions to select generators for service. A competitive auction essentially takes all offers, orders them from least-cost to highest-cost, and then moves up the supply curve to select exactly the amount of energy needed for that operating interval.

Competition to provide economic value results in a direct benefit to society. It tends to conserve the social costs required to provide a social benefit. The notion of competition that is carrying forward to the utility of the future is that each entity competing in the wholesale or retail markets will aim to keep costs low so that prices will also be low. Further, a competitor will tend to keep its profit margin as modest as possible to further reduce the chance of pricing itself out of the market. This is the idealized model of competitive markets, where individual players enter the market at prices close to their marginal costs, and the prices that clear the market tend to reflect the marginal cost of supply.

Rent-seeking competition is different. In economics, "rent" can be anything that brings in money without directly returning new value to society. Patents and copyrights are a form of economic rent, in that they enable a sort of taxation on the subsequent use of inventions and ideas after those innovations have been created and become capable of providing economic value to society. The ability to enjoy the reward of rent in the form of intellectual property protection provides an economic incentive for the creation of new inventions and ideas. But the rent itself— the royalty payment—pays for an already extant item of value, not a new one.

While intellectual property rents can provide indirect benefit to society, other types of rent-seeking activities do not. Market manipulation, for example, is strategic behavior that manufactures extraordinary conditions in the market that otherwise would not have occurred. It results in an exaggerated transfer of wealth—from consumers who are unaware of these new conditions, and are therefore powerless to respond, into the pockets of those who artificially caused those conditions to occur.

This type of malignant rent-seeking activity emerged as a serious threat to wholesale restructuring in major electricity markets in the late 1990s and early 2000s. California's early attempt at restructuring provides the best example of how this type of rent-seeking activity can occur—and how devastating it can be. Companies such as Enron spent considerable effort examining the new market's rules for scheduling and bidding. Some of the strategies Enron executed involved creating the appearance of line congestion through its day-ahead scheduling practices, and then dispatching its resources in real time so that it was paid for relieving the congestion it had caused on paper. Other strategies involved arbitraging power flows between areas where prices were capped and areas where they were not. Not only did the transactions provide no new value to the market, the economic transfers resulting from artificially high prices drove a major customer-serving utility into bankruptcy and jeopardized many others. The operational decisions needed to secure these rents took generators out of the supply mix for strategic periods of time, sometimes resulting in rolling blackouts across the state.

The lesson for the utility of the future is that socially beneficial competition does not happen on its own. Among the diversity of profit maximizers that constitute the competitive market, there will be some who perceive their well-being largely in terms of rent-seeking activity. Among rent seekers there will be an even smaller group whose rent-seeking is not only devoid of social value but is in fact pathological.

Regulators take on a new role under competition: the economic police walking the beat of the marketplace. Where their old role in the regulatory contract was to approve specific expenditures, and set prices paid by all customers, the regulators' new role is to monitor market activity so that those who play by the rules can determine their own reasonable prices and have a fair shot at competitive success. The State will need the information and expertise to distinguish market manipulation from legitimate strategy, along with enforcement authority to punish pathological rent-seeking.

The Federal Energy Regulatory Commission (FERC) formalized this distinction when it introduced the concept of market-based rate authority. Its traditional regulatory model, replicated by state regulatory authorities everywhere, was cost-of-service regulation. Rates in the cost-of-service model were determined by the regulator after a review of all costs that were permissible for rate recovery. Market-based rates were different, however. FERC would grant authority for the market participants to set their own rates provided that the market was sufficiently competitive. The regulator's main task is to evaluate market conditions to ensure that no market participant can exercise market power.

Of all the lessons that wholesale market restructuring bequeaths to the utility of the future, competition is the one that provides the most instructive window into how the electric sector is changing. While California's experience in 2000 shows how damaging a handful of pathological rent seekers can be, overall the process of restructuring demonstrates the potential benefit of competition for the creation of value. Competition happens in a conditioned economic environment, and the type of competition that arises depends on the conditions in that environment. The challenge is to encourage the conditions that foster competition for the creation of value, and to close the loopholes that lead to market manipulation and other forms of pathological rent seeking.

Price Signals, Part 2

Price signals are to the utility of the future what nerve impulses are to a healthy body. Just as a back ache communicates the need for some adjustment in position or activity somewhere else on the body, so too should a costly inefficiency create signals that trigger an appropriate adjustment. Behaviors that increase the cost of providing power should be more expensive to the person engaging in that behavior. Those that save money should return some of the savings to the person responsible for the benefit. The entire mass of price signals should be reliable enough to support new investment when new infrastructure is needed.

Cost causation is the driving principle behind healthy price signals. This means actions need to be specific, time-limited, and attributable to the market participant. It also means that the action must be valued properly so that the commensurate cost or savings can be assigned. This enables the price signal to incentivize or discourage the behavior to the degree valued by the market.

Not all actions are easily assigned to specific players, however. Some costs need to be socialized across the entire market, because they provide shared social benefits. Transmission and distribution infrastructure must be sufficient for the electricity market to work at all, so these costs are usually socialized across all end users. Some ancillary services, such as frequency response, voltage control, and special generation services to recover from a system blackout, are deployed based on system conditions that are not attributable to any specific user. This makes individual or differentiated price signals inappropriate, so these services, too, are socialized.

On the other hand, the cost of producing electricity varies throughout the day. A customer using large amounts of electricity during peak hours will therefore be causing more production cost than another customer using the same amount of electricity during off-peak hours. Varying retail prices to reflect the difference in cost between peak and off-peak hours sends an economic signal to end users that rewards shifting load from peak to off-peak. This results in greater efficiency in the operation of the grid and savings throughout the economy that can be applied elsewhere.[40]

Switching a coal or natural gas generator from "off" to "on" takes time and money. Equipment needs to be checked, boilers need to be prepared for pressurization, steam and fuel lines need to be tested, and many other procedures must be completed before the actual generation of electricity can begin. Once the unit is started, the machinery needs to operate at a minimum level to avoid damage to the equipment. Thus, the basic decision to commit a generator for availability leads to sunk costs even before it produces the first megawatt-hour of energy.

Once the unit is committed, most of the additional costs are related to how much energy the machine generates. Two factors determine the cost of producing one more megawatt-hour of energy: the cost of fuel and the generator's heat rate (the efficiency with which the generator converts one Btu of heat into one kilowatt-hour of electricity). The unit's efficiency is seldom constant, however. Pushing the machine from 99% of its output capacity to full output capacity normally requires more heat (and therefore more fuel) than moving from 50% to 51%.

All these costs translate to a generator's offer price curve—a set of megawatt quantities based on the unit's level of generation, with each point paired with a minimum payment that the unit's owner is willing to accept for operating at the given level. The RTO auction selects the least cost set of generators and op-

---

[40]Some actions might result in greater use of these socially pooled resources above what is normally required to maintain reliability. Price signals and penalties can provide economic incentives to individual market participants to avoid unusually high reliance on these services, even if the cost of normal use is socialized.

erating levels needed to meet demand, and the price of the last offer selected sets the clearing price for the whole market.[41]

These prices provide a decision signal to the generator's owner. Tomorrow's prices might be unknown, but the owner does know where the break point is between operating at a loss and full recovery of costs. Energy dispatch and the procurement of capacity for ancillary services are both done by auction, so the owner can decide the minimum day-ahead price point needed for committing the unit and then offer the unit into the market at or above that price level.

Besides the basic decisions about energy dispatch and ancillary service procurement, RTO rules also include penalties for violations that make operating the grid more difficult and costly. Some are also exploring distinct markets for special high-value ancillary services. Price signals run all throughout an organized wholesale market

Agents that monitor RTO activity have annual reports that review the previous operating year and test whether price outcomes were reasonably close to overall market conditions of scarcity or surplus. These regular reports have two objectives: (1) to investigate whether high prices are the result of manipulation or market power abuse and (2) to identify the need for improvements in market rules that can ensure market outcomes—prices —are truly indicative of system-wide scarcity or surplus. High prices *per se* do not raise market concerns, provided that the investigation shows them to be in response to legitimate scarcity. Price spikes that are the result of deliberate and strategic withholding by a supplier with enough market share to cause prices to increase are a concern, however, because they arise from a scarcity that is manufactured.

---

[41] In most markets, the clearing price also takes into account transmission congestion and the cost of re-dispatching generators to avoid overloading any lines. This causes clearing prices to differentiate by location, based on the system cost of adding one more megawatt of demand at a given system node.

Well-tempered price signals have characteristics that increase their ability to incentivize appropriate actions. These characteristics include transparency, alacrity, and stability.

Transparency

If prices are indeed to be a signal, people whose behaviors cause system costs to change must be able to see them (or at least anticipate them) in time to adapt their behaviors. The whole point of price signals is to affect the decisions that individuals make and to push those decisions in the direction of greater efficiency. Prices, therefore, need to inform individuals' decision-making thought processes.

"Gotcha" pricing—charging an individual after-the-fact for a behavior that a person did not know was causing excessive cost or harm—provides no meaningful signal for economic choices. This is counterproductive to economic efficiency and social welfare in two ways. First, it means that inefficient behavior that could have been modifies remains unchanged. This inefficiency can potentially affect all of society. Second, it can result in a socially useless transfer of wealth (a so-called "deadweight" loss). The non-signal of this kind of higher price simply taxes the individual participating in the market as an incremental cost that provides no additional measure of benefit.

Transparency also extends to the mechanisms that form prices. When wholesale market participants in RTOs can see in detail the energy prices that affect their business operations, they can form strategies accordingly. There is also a psychological benefit to transparency. Higher market confidence in pricing mechanisms makes risk assessment more robust, and better risk assessment improves decisions made in the market.

Alacrity

The speed at which price signals form should be commensurate with the speed at which market participants can change related behavior. If prices are sticky—that is, the prices change at a slower pace than the phenomena causing prices to change—the signals can be mixed. Prices that are slow to change can end up incentivizing the right behaviors at the wrong times, or vice versa.

Consider, for example, a price component based on the customer's peak demand level. This is a per-kilowatt or per-megawatt charge based on the customer's highest level of demand during the billing period. A demand charge can be structured in such a way as to economically discourage a sudden surge in the amount of electricity used. This can be done by ratcheting up to a higher rate per kilowatt if at some point during the billing period the instantaneous demand exceeds a certain kilowatt threshold. The longer the per-kilowatt charge remains at this higher rate, the less incentive the customer has to adopt energy management measures that would keep demand below the threshold level. The efficiency measures might work to reduce demand, but the customer's reward would be diminished.

Another potential problem is price chasing. This was one of the features of the early California market that Enron and others were able to manipulate in 2000 and 2001. Some wholesale prices moved in response to market signals, while others did not. A market participant that could move financial commitments from one asset to another or from one market space to another could "play" the changes in price differences to secure the kind of pathological rents described earlier in this chapter.

On the retail side, advanced meters will significantly increase the end-use customer's ability to respond to timely price signals. This is a major contrast with conventional meters that only measure how many kilowatt-hours flowed during the billing month but provide no data on the time the consumption occurred.

Stability

Another important function of market prices is to signal the need for new capital investment. These long-term decisions essentially boil down to whether future revenues for the proposed investment are likely to be sufficient to meet both the project's day-to-day operating costs and the long-term fixed costs of financing the project.

Investment in new infrastructure such as a generator or a transmission line takes time—time for planning and permitting, and time for convincing potential investors and lenders that market conditions will support a major capital investment. Once built, the new infrastructure needs to have a flow of revenue sufficient to cover both its cost of operation and the fixed payments needed under the project's capital structure. These time requirements impose a "gestation" period on capital formation. The relevant market prices during the capital gestation period need to be sufficiently stable for a prudent assessment of risk. Stable prices tend to reduce risk, narrow the band of plausible future financial conditions, and extend the time horizon over which developers and investors can see through the fog of future uncertainty.

Thus, price stability is crucial to capital formation in a competitive market. Under the old regulatory contract, the stability of revenue was guaranteed by the State through the granting of a monopoly franchise (which prevented revenue leakage due to customer defections) and setting service charges at a level that ensured the utility a reasonable rate of return on its investments. When fragmentation disrupts the assumptions underlying the regulatory contract and competition becomes the paradigm, however, the burden for informing future investment decisions falls to market prices. The absolute stability of the regulatory process is replaced by the relative stability of prices, where the degree of price volatility is a key variable in measuring financial risk.

Both supply and demand need to be systematic enough to form a meaningful price signal and an effective market response. This does not mean that supply and demand need to be constant. If the major factors that cause changes are understood and predictable or can be mitigated, the variations can to some extent be approached systematically and can thereby be rationalized. If either side of the equation lacks stability, the price signals become moving targets to which market participants can formulate no rational, economically beneficial response.

Price signals that form predictably and systematically can achieve stability even if they change rapidly. It is not necessary for behaviors to change moment-to-moment, provided that each tick upward or downward is predictably related to a particular decision or response that the supplier or the customer can control consistently. The underlying stability of highly granular changes can be synthesized into a consolidated price signal that will both simplify the signal and maintain its integrity with respect to the factors causing it.

What Fragmentation Looks Like

The foregoing—the role of the market maker, competition that is fair, and meaningful price signals—are *sine qua non* to ensuring that fragmentation unfolds in a manner that supports the public interest. Without these prerequisites, the so-called "market" would be nothing more than chaos, in which capital formation would be virtually impossible and blackouts common. With them, creative destruction and the public interest are harmonized with the greatest economic efficiency toward the greatest level of social fulfillment.

Healthy fragmentation on the supply side tends to reduce the cost of generation because suppliers—through the market maker—compete head-to-head to be included in dispatch for the next day or hour. In the Texas wholesale market, 80% of the generation capacity is dispersed among twenty-five different companies, none of which owns more than 14% of the market's total capacity. In PJM, the largest U.S. RTO, sixteen different companies own 80% of all generation capacity, with no share larger than 12%.[42] There has been a learning curve certainly, but trends in retail rates from about 2006 onward indicate a split between restructured markets and monopoly utilities. Retail rates have fallen by about 1% per year in areas where the wholesale market has been restructured. In Texas, where both the wholesale and retail markets have been restructured since 2002, inflation-adjusted retail prices fell by 4% per year between 2006 and 2015. This contrasts starkly with the Southeast and the Mountain states—still served by vertically integrated monopoly utilities—where rates increased by 1% annually.[43]

With fragmentation comes a proliferation of parallel relationships between supply and demand. When a monopoly utility is the sole supplier and sole retailer serving demand, there is essentially only one supply-demand relationship. Some traditional utilities have made efforts towards serving differentiated demand (providing options for all-renewable service, for example), and this is to their credit. But the lack of supply diversity nevertheless

---

[42] Based on annual generator capacity data compiled by the U.S. Energy Information Administration (EIA), using 2015 as the sample year. In both cases, the remaining capacity is distributed among dozens of smaller owners.

[43] Based on state average retail prices compiled by the EIA. There are, of course, many reasons why prices change, some of which relate either directly or indirectly to the changes wrought by restructuring. For example, lower natural gas prices have helped push more of the generation mix toward gas. In restructured wholesale markets like Texas, New England, and the Middle Atlantic where merchant generation has flourished, the use of security-constrained economic dispatch has greatly helped to make optimal use of the opportunities for cost saving.

limits how far these efforts can go.[44] The utility as sole supplier has no incentive toward risky service innovations, because at the very least, such changes set off alarms from the utility's regulator. With fragmentation, a company that serves retail customers makes its own supply arrangements—sometimes contracting with specific generators and sometimes settling for "system" power that is dispatched generally by the RTO. This results in a web of relationships between many generators and many retailers. The diverse strands of this web make it possible to differentiate supply arrangements on the wholesale side according to customer demand on the retail side with far more detail than a monopoly utility could provide.

Stable price signals on the supply side enable innovation by entrepreneurs on the retail side of this new web of commercial relationships. If supply, demand, and their resulting price signals settle into systematic hourly patterns, retail providers can design variable rate services that create savings both for the customer and the provider. For instance, in some fragmented retail markets, providers offer programs where late-night use or weekend use is free. Fragmentation allows innovators to test ideas, some of which work and some of which do not. But in a fragmented market, the burden of failure, like the reward of success, rests solely with the entrepreneur taking the risk. Society has no obligation to clean up the mess if a retail idea fails to attract customers.

With supply fragmentation implemented in a stable manner, retail demand can begin participating in the wholesale market in

---

[44] Utility "green power" offerings are a good example. Most customers in Colorado are served by a vertically integrated utility, which offers a 100% wind power option to its customers. Colorado has excellent wind resources, as does Texas which operates as a competitive wholesale and retail market. Colorado customers who in 2017 opted for the utility's wind power program paid a premium of 1.5 cents per kilowatt-hour. In Texas at that same time, where more than a dozen retail providers were competing to offer all-renewable service, the typical mark-up was less than half a cent per kilowatt-hour, with some products priced even lower.

ways it never could before. This is because price signals that reflect the marginal value of generating power will simultaneously signal the value of not consuming power. Take, for example, a large industrial operation that uses several megawatts of power throughout the day, but with sufficient notice can take a 10-megawatt operation off-line. By calculating its cost of deferring operations for a few hours, this industrial user can submit an offer into the market for the next day. If the price of energy clears at a higher price than the industrial user's cost of deferring production, the company will be paid for *not* using 10 megawatts of power it otherwise would have used. From the perspective of the power system, this is the same as generating 10 more megawatts of power if the industrial user had continued to operate normally.

The complicated business of enabling demand resources to participate in the market is an important role filled by the market maker, because without an objective platform for measuring and validating information, market-valued wholesale demand response is problematic. When it works, the wholesale market fragments further due to the number of new resources (in this case, "virtual" generators in the form of systematic load reduction) competing economically to provide power. Competition deepens.

The better price signals are up and down the supply chain, the easier it is for customers large to fully inhabit their new role in the future utility: that of being producers and consumers simultaneously. Arizona, Colorado, California, and Minnesota struggled to reconcile these dual roles in the context of monopoly utilities in their efforts to accommodate rooftop solar power installed by residential customers. The problem is that without time-sensitive price signals that accurately capture the difference between the value of producing electricity and the cost of using it, payments to customer-generators necessarily become simplistic and inaccurate.[45]

Failing to get price signals right—or even worse, not paying attention to them at all—can doom grid modernization efforts. The California market failed in 2000 and 2001 because the fragmentation it introduced was dysfunctional. Price signals in the new wholesale market were gibberish. They violated all the principles of good pricing described earlier in this chapter, and instead were the result of rent-seeking behaviors that manipulated conditions to manufacture (and get revenue from) the appearance of scarcity.[46] Other markets have learned from the California experience and have taken steps to ensure restructuring is conducive to healthy, socially productive competition.

Market fragmentation does not mean a free-for-all, however. Participants in the market—retail as well as wholesale—need to have a basic level of business competence. Generation owners need to know how to communicate with the RTO or other market maker real-time and must have the financial wherewithal to settle obligations at the end of the operating day. Retail service providers need to demonstrate their ability to secure power supplies and must also have the financial wherewithal to settle accounts at the end of the operating day. It is the State's job to set

---

[45] This is the only economically valid way to reconcile the conflicts that are arising in the distributed generation space, especially for rooftop PV. A neighborhood with significant rooftop PV deployment should be equivalent to a single utility-scale PV installation, where production is valued and paid just as any other wholesale supplier is paid. Because the value of solar goes beyond the commodity electricity that is produced, the market needs to provide the right economic signals for the right application of solar to occur. Without it, valuing and paying for rooftop solar becomes a crapshoot, risking underpayment to the customers who install the systems or overpayment by the rest of society.

[46] Certainly, California experienced some legitimate scarcity in the summer months, because drought had reduced the amount of energy the state normally got from hydroelectric resources. This natural shortage left the market defenseless against the pathological rent-seeking and manipulation that occurred.

standards of entry that have the force of law. The purpose of entry prerequisites is not necessarily to protect unqualified actors from their own mistakes but to reduce the likelihood of economic carnage due to bankruptcy or other failure. It is the market maker's job to enforce these standards in a nondiscriminatory manner.

Persistence of Virtual Monopoly Conditions

So far in this chapter we have been discussing the process of fragmentation—what drives it and how it works in a direction that furthers the public interest. Fragmentation is the dissolution of natural monopoly. But the dissolution, if allowed to evolve naturally, can play out differently and in some circumstances, might not happen at all. Conditions in a sector can persist that maintain monopoly as the virtual state of the electricity business in that sector.

While competition is in the public interest, it is never in the public interest for policy and institutions to pretend competition is happening when it is not. If the relevant market space is not large enough or robust enough to sustain competition, if conditions prohibit the formation of meaningful price signals through the intersection of supply and demand, or if the market is too dissolute for market-driven capital formation, then a region's electricity sector could remain a virtual monopoly.

As discussed in Chapter 2, it can be useful to regard natural monopoly and virtual monopoly as endpoints on a *continuum* of institutional characteristics. The continuum is useful because natural monopoly as defined by economists does not get the discussion where it needs to be, even after considering the wide diversity of opinion among economists on the matter. Distinguishing between natural and virtual, or effective, monopoly allows delving into questions that are more fundamental to the public interest.

118

The first area where these questions should be posed is the breadth and depth of demand. This refers to both the volume of demand for a service, and the diversity of preferences bound up within that volume of demand. An expansive and robustly competitive market space allows opportunities for entrepreneurial innovation. There is a hunger for more choices, and the demand around for each choice is large enough for an innovative provider to achieve some degree of economy of scale.

Conversely, the shallower and less diverse the pool of demand is, the more limited the opportunities are for competition. Launching and maintaining an enterprise (either for electricity generation or for providing the billing and customer service necessary for retailing) involves real costs that are apart from the commodity electricity being produced or sold. If the customer base is small, it will be more difficult for new competitors to enter the market. If the market is too small, entry will simply not make economic sense.

The U.S. power sector itself provides a meaningful illustration of the effects. The regions served by organized wholesale power markets constituted about 50% of the country's land area geographically in 2017, but they accounted for more than 60% of the nation's electricity consumption and production. The areas that have been less inclined to move away from vertically integrated monopolies are those where demand for electricity is not as concentrated.

The corporate culture of the incumbent utilities can also come into play. Operating as a regulated monopoly is a model of business operation fundamentally different from competing in a contestable market; it's not how utilities are used to operating. But an important factor is that many of these markets are too small to be contestable in any practical sense.

One interesting sub-theme of electric industry restructuring in the early 2000s was the situation that arose in smaller markets. In these markets, there was often very little discussion of competition. "Deregulation" was the public focus, often riding parasitically on the more ideological theme that any government intervention stifled innovation and led to economic inefficiency. Not surprisingly, the incumbent utilities in these public debates were often in favor of "deregulation"—especially if the countervailing hammers of divestiture, unbundling, and market power mitigation were not on the table.

In fact, restructuring from cost-of-service regulation to a truly competitive market demands a lot from the utility and from the State. It involves renegotiating and rewriting the regulatory contract in a way that takes both parties into new socioeconomic territory. Whether there is an increase in social welfare at the end of these trials depends in part on whether the fundamental elements of competition are present and on whether the State is willing to certify the new institutions needed to keep competition robust and open.

Conclusion

Mass-produced electricity no longer needs to be a vertically integrated enterprise. Restructuring has proved that power generation, delivery, and retail customer service can be unbundled into separate business enterprises, and that some services nowadays can be provided by multiple competitors. Improvements in information technology raise the possibility of even more granular fragmentation reaching as far as the individual retail customer.

Distribution—the delivery of electricity from the transmission system to end-use customers—is where monopoly conditions are most likely to persist. This resembles conditions of the early days of electric power, because one facet of the technology that has not changed is the need to have wires leading to the customers' points of use.[47] Thus while vertical monopolies have little room in the utility of the future, horizontal monopolies within the distribution segment could persist.

For both generation and retail sales, however, the key economic characteristic of fragmentation is competition. But competition is seldom perfect. A shock could create conditions in the market that change faster than the system's ability to respond. A rent-seeking profit maximizer could succeed in gaming the rules and causing significant distortions in the market. Numerous flaws could conspire to reduce the transparency, alacrity, and stability of price signals in the market.

Yet these are puzzles to be solved, and not necessarily showstopping problems. While no market is perfect, it is just as true that any market can be made better. The factors described in the previous sections of this chapter all point to conditions that can be monitored and nurtured. Some degree of market organization is essential if competition in a fragmented electricity sector is to work. This necessitates a new public interest role for the market maker and for the State.

---

[47] Off-grid customers would not worry about the utility distribution system, but I would argue that they have little influence on the distribution utility one way or another. From the utility's perspective, a customer going off grid eliminates both revenue and cost with one generally cancelling out the other. In any case, being off the grid has always been an option.

Chapter 5: Customer Liberation

Everyone dresses the same. Eats the same food. Attends the same entertainment. Lives in the same kind of home. Reads the same books. Follows the same schedule. The only choice is whether to conform or become so divorced from the rest of society that one might as well be on a deserted island.

This scenario is a far cry from the world of diversity we enjoy in real life. Human beings thrive psychologically on choice. Options exercise the intellect. How each person exercises options helps form that individual. The freedom to make economic choices is an important dimension of well-rounded human expression.

For most of the electric industry's commercial existence, being a residential customer was to be a human unit without self-defining choice. The utility recognized (and billed) virtually no nuance in consumer behavior. Several obscure charges might appear on the monthly bill, but none represented a choice and all of them were calculated in much the same way: per kilowatt-hour based on the same number of kilowatt-hours used. A customer simply used more or less of the same generic commodity, and that was it.

This simplicity was convenient for the utility as well as its regulators. It made commercial sense a century ago when electricity service itself was a novelty. Over time, however, the consumer economy has developed more and increasingly diverse ways of providing customers with value, convenience, and leisure through the use of electricity. Differences in household income contribute to different desires for energy efficiency. And as people become more aware of how the electricity they use affects the natural environment, many become more concerned about how the electricity they use is generated.

One of the most radical and exciting features of the future utility is the liberation of end-use customers—especially residential customers—from the confines of standardization. Just as information is dissolving the foundations of natural monopoly, information is empowering choice. Choice is the demand-side corollary of the institutional fragmentation happening on the electricity sector's supply side.

Liberation is not just about the new things customers *can* do with more technology, however. A utility that deploys smart grid capabilities but makes no meaningful change in how it bills for service could end up wasting millions. The features brought by new technology are economically relevant only if they open new sources of tangible value for the customer. "Cool" is not enough. The utility and its regulators must consider *why* and *how* a customer would find value in the new features. A customer can choose to be more or less efficient in using electricity. The societal value of such customer liberation is in being able to change behaviors in the direction of greater efficiency. The value to the individual is to enjoy lower electricity costs.

Customers will be on a learning curve just as much as utilities themselves will be. For one thing, retail customers have seldom needed to distinguish between the work value of electricity (that is, the things that happen when the customer plugs something in and turns it on) and its reliability value (all the things that happen elsewhere on the grid so that the electricity will actually be there when the customer needs it to be regardless of when the switch is turned on). When customers all predictably behave the same way, bundling the cost of reliability and the cost of producing the commodity electricity into one simple, uniform rate is easy. When usage patterns start to diverge, however, keeping the same rate structure can result in some customers overpaying for reliability and others underpaying. Thus, matching behavior with prices will inevitably end up lowering some customers' bills and increasing others' because reliability will become its own value proposition. Before, customers never had to worry about how to value reliability. In the utility of the future, they will.

Choice will therefore be both a freedom and a burden, with the customer ultimately deciding whether to embrace it. Those who would rather focus their economic attention on other decisions may choose a default electricity service that looks much like it does today. In doing so, they might forfeit potential savings in favor of convenience and simplicity. In an environment of customer liberation, choosing not to choose could be a rational economic decision for some customers. The crucial point is that simplicity is not forced on consumers who prefer choice.

Customer liberation will be noisy. A growing diversity of preferences will be met with a growing diversity of entrepreneurs responding to new market opportunities, making retail electricity service a bustling bazaar. That is far different from the staid model of retail service provided by the traditional utility. But if the aim of policy makers, regulators, and utilities is to anticipate what the future could look like and to smooth the path of transition for the public, this is the end state they need to keep in mind.

This chapter develops three areas within the theme of customer liberation: what drives customer choice; what constrains customer choice; and what role the retail market maker will play in this customer liberation. Most of this chapter will focus on residential customers and small businesses and on methods of institutional organization—*tekhnología*—that enable them greater choice in electric service. Large commercial operations and industrial users already enjoy some measure of price-sensitive choice, and these models provide some guidance for what is possible for individuals. In fact, one driver for the existing degree of choice for larger customers is their diversity of needs and preferences. The thesis of this chapter is that individual electricity customers are realizing their own diversity, albeit on a smaller scale. One of the adventures of the future utility will be learning how to liberate this diversity of individual preferences.

The Complexity of Consumer Preferences

To see how customer liberation works, let's start with the basic concept of consumer preference. A consumer's interest in a given good or service is a function of the value the consumer derives from it. The value can be the satisfaction of a necessity such as food—or increasingly in mainstream society—access to electricity. A need-driven value tends to be economically inelastic relative to its price, meaning that the individual will place the same value on the same amount of the good or service regardless of what it costs.

Things that are in the "want it" bucket tend to be more elastic in value than things in the "need it" bucket. For instance, housing (a mortgage payment or a rent payment) might be the first thing a person pays each month because the need for shelter is so inelastic, but going to movies or dining out are leisure activities that could easily expand or shrink depending on disposable income.

Value is also a matter of perception. The customer's familiarity with the product is important, but perception can also depend on external factors such as the customer's history, income, stock of existing wealth, expectations, tastes, and social values. To further complicate things, any factor affecting the consumer's perception of value can vary over time. Sending a child to college, receiving a bonus at work, changing jobs—these are all circumstances that affect perceived value, resulting in a stewpot of preferences that is extremely dynamic. If the perceived value seems consistently greater than the price, the consumer will have a notion of being better off by taking the deal.

When this individual microeconomic decision process is translated to the macroeconomic level, the process is replicated across thousands and perhaps millions of individuals consumers.

At this level, the decision is not a discrete purchase decision, but is instead a distribution of decisions. The price of the good or service may be fixed, but because each consumer brings to the proposition a different sense of personal value and economic awareness, the market response to the price becomes a rather fuzzy probability distribution.

This is what choice looks like from a macroeconomic perspective for just one good or service. When considered as a household budget exercise, even the individual decision becomes more complex. The choice, in fact, goes well beyond whether to choose the given good or service. Rather, it is how the cost and value of that decision compares to other parallel decisions. The deal in question might be good, but if it can be substituted with another good or service that provides more value at a lower price, the decision might change. Temporary personal circumstances also come into play, too. A salesman might persuade a customer that buying a new dining room set is a good value, but if the same customer were moving or downsizing, the salesman would likely fail to persuade.

Complexity grows exponentially once this multidimensional microeconomic process spreads across the entire market and becomes a macroeconomic phenomenon. When the complexity of demand meets a cadre of entrepreneurs, a normal consumer market responds through product differentiation. Preferences will over time cluster into coherent threads of demand, and a large market might reveal many distinct demand threads. The producer's challenge is to find the right mix of product offerings to meet these demands.

The ability to deal with a diversity of consumer preferences is a major difference between the utility of the past and the utility of the future. Monopolies seldom bothered about diversity, because they had neither the need nor the incentive to do so. The product they provided was essential and had no practical substitute, so the monopoly utility faced no threat of losing customers or revenue.

The utility of the future will be different. The increasing diversity of consumer preferences is dovetailing with another important change: Delivering retail service to customers is one part of the electricity supply chain that is no longer a natural monopoly. As retail markets change to accommodate choice, the pressure cooker of pent-up demand for diversity will find opportunities for satisfaction. However, this won't happen at the same pace in every market, because larger markets will tend to have a mix of diversity and depth.

The next sections take up the question of what this newly diversified demand will look like. Market experience has shown a few of the points on which customers exhibit distinct preferences. Prices and the natural economic tendency to prefer lower cost run throughout all of them; therefore, the integrity of price signals will be just as important on the retail side of the equation. After looking at the matter of choice points and price signals, I'll then look at how entrepreneurs might meet this new demand through the development of "buyers clubs" that aggregate customers with similar patterns of demand. Finally, I will describe how the market maker and the State can work together to make choice workable and beneficial to society overall.

Choice Points

Chapter 2 examined the public interest value of enabling customer choice, without delving into the microeconomic factors that would shape how customers choose. Given a diversity of preferences in balancing an array of economic values, society will tend toward greater fulfillment in an environment of choice than it would be without choice.

It is difficult to predict where the right to choose might take customer preferences for electricity service. Certainly, some choice points have already emerged in markets where some degree of retail choice is possible. However, a fully liberated market will likely offer more choices in the future. Predicting what those future choices might be is not the point of this book nor is it necessary to do so. One of the defining characteristics of the future utility is an economic environment conducive to service innovation. As long as the utility can accommodate entrepreneurial innovation with respect to retail service, there is no need to limit the possibilities by predicting what they will be.

The most important choice points from the standpoint of economic theory are those that link behavior and choices on the demand side (that is, retail customers) with costs and operational decisions on the supply side. These types of choice points have the greatest potential for channeling the impulses of customer liberation in ways that reduce the social cost of providing electricity.

Two choice points have emerged so far—clean energy and price-adaptive usage for achieving aggressive savings. Accommodating these choices will mean different social roles and different business models for the utility.

Clean Energy

One of the first points of customer choice has been the selection of service derived from renewable energy. In Houston and Dallas, for example, where the electricity markets have been restructured at both the retail and wholesale levels, customers can shop from among more than eighty all-renewable electricity service plans offered by dozens of providers. Even in some markets still served by monopoly utilities, customers have the option for all-wind or all-solar electricity service which the utility manages through its own electricity supplies. First, however, it might be useful to review some basic concepts about how the grid works physically, economically, and socially.

Unless a person is living completely off-grid, electricity is a pooled social resource that is managed as an aggregated mass.

The sum of electrons added to the pool (from any source) equals the sum of electrons taken from it (for any usage).[48] The grid itself is both a common reservoir of energy and a means of conveying energy from all generation points to all points of usage. Energy in and energy out are metered, so that at the end of the day accountants can financially settle how much each customer is charged for what it took from the energy pool and how much each generator is paid for what it put into the pool.

From the grid's physical perspective, there are no "green" and no "dirty" electrons. Just as molecules of water from a well are indistinguishable from molecules from a stream once they are in the reservoir and eventually piped out and delivered to the public, electrons carry no imprint of how they were generated. There is no physical path by which electricity generated at a wind turbine flows exclusively to a customer who chooses wind-powered electricity. But the accounting system that overlays the physical system keeps track of where electricity comes from and where it goes. Thus, when retail customers buy renewable power, their transactions economically cause more renewable energy to be added to the grid's energy pool than would be otherwise. Their action on the demand side is linked financially with actions on the supply side, such that renewable generation replaces generation from fossil fuels with respect to the amount of electricity those customers take from the grid.

Maintaining the integrity of the accounting system is therefore an important task for both the market maker and the regulator in the future electricity sector. The previous chapter introduced and described the market maker; the next chapter will address in greater depth the role of the regulator in the utility of the future. Here, the point is that if customers are to make economic choices with respect to electricity service, they need to

---

[48] Some amount is naturally lost in the transmission of electricity between the point of generation and the point of use. These system loss factors add to the socialized costs of grid management.

have confidence that the grid and its associated system of accounting can make good on that choice. This includes putting in place a credible method for certifying that customers get what they pay for when choosing all-renewable electricity service.

Most states have instituted renewable energy content requirements in the form of a renewable portfolio standard (RPS). These requirements set a social minimum for renewable energy use. Thus, if the RPS is 30%, then every customer's electric service will have a renewable content of at least 30% because the aggregated pool of electricity used to supply that service will be at least 30%. If a customer buys service that is 100% renewable, the service provider secures the obligatory amount of renewable power required by the RPS, with the balance coming from additional wind, solar or other renewables that are not being used anywhere else for the basic RPS requirement. One way to visualize the accounting is that demand for all-renewable service permanently diverts a portion of the renewable energy supply stream away from the RPS. This draw-down of the supply pool creates a temporary scarcity with respect to maintaining the social standard created by the RPS. The scarcity is temporary because it creates an economic signal for the development of new renewables.

Public policy may require the utility of the future to maintain a social minimum for renewable energy content. Customer preferences for renewable energy will be diverse, however, which means that no single RPS requirement will represent a level satisfactory to all customers. In an environment of customer liberation, individuals who want to do better than average do not have to wait for the State to act. They can exercise choice immediately, creating their own critical mass of demand that will lead to supply effects.

In some states, community solar gardens are evolving as a means of customer choice for clean power. Solar panels are located not on the roof of an individual warehouse, store, or residence, but at a consolidated site that can accommodate a larger installation. A customer can buy a share of the solar garden, with that share of the facility's monthly production credited to the customer's bill. While the electricity itself flows onto the grid and is pooled operationally with all other generation resources managed by the utility, the meter at the facility's point of interconnection enables the utility to do the accounting to accurately credit the kilowatt-hours produced to the solar garden's participating owners. The solar garden takes advantage of economies of scale (cost per kilowatt installed can be lower than that of solar installed on an individual roof). It makes direct-owned solar accessible to those living in apartments, condominiums, and other types of housing where individual rooftop solar is not practical; and the ownership can easily follow the customer who moves from one apartment to another.

As clean power grows into a commercially coherent choice point, a more defined economic space for price competition will emerge. An economic preference for renewables in no way excludes an economic preference for low-cost options. One feature of models such as solar gardens and all-renewable electricity service is that they are accounting innovations that adapt to the physical realities of the grid's hardware. An entrepreneur who is knowledgeable about operations, financial settlement processes, and customer demand possibilities will have an incentive to find low-cost ways to satisfy this demand niche.

Price Adaptive Usage

In some areas where the new utility paradigm has taken hold, residential customers have a bold new choice for time-of-use service: free at night and on weekends. This allows customers the opportunity to pursue aggressive cost reduction by changing their usage patterns.

Two points are important here. First is the evolution of the basic time-of-use (TOU) billing model. TOU rates are based on the fact that the incremental cost of energy during the day and especially during peak hours is higher than at other times of the day. If advanced meters are widespread throughout the service territory, the utility can measure when a customer is using more or less electricity. Rates on a TOU service can then be set based on the actual incremental cost of power at different times of the day, providing the customer with a mild price signal for shifting usage to off-peak hours.

This is a step in the right direction for the conventional monopoly utility. But to a great extent it is still an old-world monopoly approach to the customer. By setting a suite of TOU rates based on the utility's incremental cost at different times of the day, the rate structure is based on a precise valuation of the utility's need. The magnitude of the price signal, however, might not be enough to incentivize a large number of customers to change how they use electricity.

This brings us to the second point: the psychological truth of uncertainty and the practical value of simplicity. Recall the earlier discussion about the complexity of consumer preferences. An individual's response to any price signal is colored by many other choices that compete not only for the same dollar but for the same minute of attention. What may appear to be a discrete response to a price signal is in fact the result of a psychological process of thoughtful consideration that, if it were visualized, would look more like a probability distribution. The less knowledge the customer has about the choice (or the less confidence a customer has in the available information), the fuzzier and more diffuse the probabilistic decision process will be. When the same signal is spread across the entire population of customers, the result can be a distribution of different responses to the same price signal.

Exaggerating the price signal skews this fuzzy psychological process more in the direction of the behavior that the price signal is intended to encourage. It introduces the possibility that the lack of response from customers who ignore the price signal will be offset somewhat by the additional response that results from over-incentivizing those who do respond. In the case of a product that is free at night or on the weekend, there is the added value of simplicity. For the retail provider, the issue is not whether each customer pays precisely according to the cost it causes, but whether the aggregation of responses across the provider's entire population of customers results in a fair and reasonable balance between total cost and total revenue. Obviously, there is additional risk for the electric provider. But it represents a sharing of the uncertainty that is inherent in the price signal.

The utility of the future will be in the business of taking risks to a much greater extent than a conventional utility does, and one place this will be seen is in the crafting of price signals to redirect customer use patterns. For the market maker, the task will be to settle wholesale costs in a manner that is fair and consistent, so that the retail provider can craft a service plan for customers that is both understandable and capable of managing the provider's financial risk.

Price Signals, Part 3

Price signals are as important at the retail level as they are at the wholesale level. Economic efficiency does not only mean making things less expensive. It also means matching services with what retail customers most value. Preferences intersect the cost of producing electricity in many complex ways, and correct prices are crucial to sorting it all out in a way that is rational, simple, and actionable.

The liberation of diverse consumer preferences will depend on price signals at the retail level that meaningfully reflect the real-time value of generation at the level of production. These signals do not need the same pin-point precision as prices at the wholesale level. Recall that unlike the single-point decision to dispatch and pay a generator, retail response takes form in thousands of decisions that are distributed in a pattern. Thus, a simple pricing plan—energy that is free after midnight, for example—can send a clear and easily understood signal to retail customers. Some will be able to adapt their usage; some will not. Those who can, such as electric vehicle owners who can recharge at home after midnight, would reduce their bills in a way that simultaneously reduces system costs by shifting demand to hours when the cost of generating electricity is considerably less. An individual customer response is not critical. What matters is whether the plan garners a coherent behavioral response from a significant number of customers. This can change how generation is dispatched systemwide.

Retail price signals will be crucial to accelerated growth of energy efficiency. In the old utility model, a customer's incentive for energy efficiency was largely limited to reducing the amount of electricity billed on the standard per-kilowatt-hour rate. The utility might have sweetened the deal with rebates on energy efficient appliances, but there were no real price signals to influence how the customer managed consumption. In the utility of the future, efficiency can be targeted with differentiated pricing intended to not only reduce the amount of energy used, but to change when it is used.

The importance of customer price signals cannot be understated. Take, for example, smart meters. These devices provide the utility with detailed information on customer usage, which when aggregated across many customers can make energy balancing, frequency response, and other reliability functions more precise and less costly. This is great for the people running the grid, but these capabilities will remain an unfulfilled promise if the investments do not give customers a reason to change their behaviors. This can *only* happen through price signals. Better visibility into customer behaviors that affect grid management means little if customers do not actually change those behaviors in a way that reduces the cost of managing reliability.

There is a corollary effect of accurate retail price signals: the end of free ridership. Take the example of home energy efficiency incentives that a utility offers to residential customers. If the utility has one common rate for all residential customers, and the program is successful enough to reduce that rate, the beneficiaries will include customers who continue to consume wastefully. With the utility of the future, charges will vary and will serve as price signals, simultaneously incentivizing cost-saving behaviors and penalizing behaviors that add to the cost of providing electricity service.

The great normalization of behavior embedded in static retail rates is another casualty of creative destruction, one likely to be most visible to retail customers of all types. The opportunities afforded by greater choice and the ability to more aggressively pursue cost savings will necessarily be balanced with penalties for cost-causing behaviors.

Aggregation through Retail Buyers Clubs

A cement factory or steel mill can bring tremendous value to grid operations with its ability to shed megawatts of load on short notice in a planned manner. Reducing load by one megawatt is just as good as one more megawatt of generation when it comes to keeping the grid in real-time balance. In many organized wholesale markets, large industrial customers with the capability of curtailing their load can compete with generating plants in offering ancillary services for grid management—and get paid for doing so at a fair, market-determined rate.

Residential customers and small businesses equipped with smart meters can provide load response, too, but individually they are usually too small to have a measurable impact. A one-kilowatt adjustment made by one small customer could easily get lost in the random load variations that occur on the grid all the time. The transaction costs—metering, calculating the price signal, monitoring and verifying the response, and providing the correct billing credit—could be so great that they outweigh the operational benefit.

On the other hand, one thousand small customers each providing one kilowatt of response at the same time can be as valuable to grid operations as one industrial customer providing one megawatt of response. This specialized retail service for coordinating the response from residential and small commercial customers, which here I refer to as *aggregation*, will be an important new feature of the future grid.

An aggregator is a third party who mediates the commercial relationship between the utility and a group of retail customers who have elected to participate in a demand response service. There are few examples of aggregation in this time of transition from the old world to the new, but the themes I've discussed throughout this book make aggregation an inevitable feature of the fully formed utility of the future. What I describe in the following paragraphs is not, therefore, a chronicle of business models in existence at this moment. Rather, I attempt to describe a generic type of business arrangement that is defined by the convergence of new economic opportunities for customers, coupled with the cleverness of entrepreneurs who find ways to leverage these opportunities into even greater benefits. By no means do I intend to show aggregation as a narrow and specific business model. As with any innovation, the forms may vary tremendously as entrepreneurs test different approaches aimed at different market segments.

Aggregation's basic elements include infrastructure and commercial relationships. All the subscribing customers need to have advanced meters that collect data in real time on usage. They also need to have telemetry on large devices such as air conditioners, refrigerators, and electric vehicle chargers that can cycle the device off and on in response to a remote signal from the aggregator.

The aggregator combines demand information for all participating customers, and acts as a single point of contact to which the utility sends a signal corresponding to the need for real-time changes in load. The utility sends one signal for demand response to the aggregator, who then breaks the signal down into many smaller signals that are relayed to all participating customers and their large-load devices. The customers' meters monitor the degree of response consistent with the price signal, and each customer receives a credit commensurate with the amount and per-unit value of response. The accounting for individual customers would be handled by the aggregator, and the utility would settle a single wholesale transaction with the aggregator based on the verified response from the aggregator's combined subscriber base.

Striking a balance between convenience and extreme cost savings in the new utility environment will often require specialized knowledge that most customers do not possess. A customer's smart meter might have copious amounts of information about usage, but knowing how to apply it to the adoption of efficient behaviors can be a steep learning curve. The aggregator can provide that specialized expertise and manage participation on behalf of the customer. Thus, aggregation can broaden the use of demand response, so that the opportunity space is no longer limited to large industrial customers and residential mansions.

Another benefit of leveraging power in numbers is that the response itself can be managed with less inconvenience to the individual customer. For example, consider a demand response for reducing load in the aggregator's client base by one megawatt for one hour. Say there are 4,000 subscribers across whom the response can be distributed, and each customer can provide an average of 1 kilowatt of load reduction. Each subscriber would only need their air conditioners, refrigerators, or car chargers turned off for 15 minutes, after which normal operation could resume.

Aggregation can provide customers—especially residential and small commercial customers—with a valuable option for balancing convenience with extreme cost savings. As the data management systems and meters become more sophisticated, both the real-time value of the service and the compensation to customers can increase. The value to customers with their own rooftop solar installations could increase even more if the systems have batteries and "smart" inverters that can also be used in demand response.

How the aggregator is paid would be addressed through the service contract with the customer, which could be as simple or as detailed as the market would bear. Information will be sufficient for the aggregator to offer a plan with a variable fee based on the actual market prices for reliability services procured by the utility from all other resources. Or the aggregator could provide a fixed-fee service in which the aggregator takes on a degree of wholesale price uncertainty in exchange for providing the subscriber a measure of retail price certainty.

This new sort of arrangement would require a particular type of regulatory oversight. Aggregators would need to demonstrate their financial capability and fiduciary responsibility prior to being certified to do business. Especially important would be the rules governing the use and maintenance of customer data. Engaging in third-party aggregation would involve the customer's consent in sharing usage information with someone other than the utility, because without that detailed information commercially meaningful aggregation would be impossible.

Finally, given the multiple information systems over which the commercially relevant information would have to travel, aggregation would also require additional measures for cybersecurity.

Customer aggregation has already taken hold in areas that have gone down the path of restructuring. In Texas and Pennsylvania, for instance, customers can take service from retail electric providers who are responsible for dealing with the system operator and distribution utility. These providers receive all the market's load-oriented price signals, particularly the differentiation in location-specific wholesale prices over the course of a day. The provider can then fashion retail product offerings for its customers that offer simple and easy-to-understand choices for usage while comporting with the detailed price signals the provider is receiving from the wholesale market. This liberates the customer from the need to follow individual price signals; the aggregator does the calculation and reduces the complexity to a simplified rate plan that, over an extended period, saves money for the customer.

In traditional markets, some regulated monopoly utilities offer residential customers incentives for installing utility-controlled thermostats and switches on air conditioners and other devices. Here, the utility itself is acting as a demand response aggregator. Compensation to the customer can be constrained by metering, however. If the customer's meter is an old model that just measures how much electricity is used but not when it is used, the utility will often offer the customer a one-time fixed payment.[49]

As information systems evolve, opening the door to third-party aggregation could become a reasonable public policy response even where utilities continue to be monopolies. The State may find it in the public interest for the utility to be a market maker as a transitional step to a future utility model. With regulatory guidance for customer protection standards and eligibility

---

[49] The biggest problem with this approach (in the context of the future utility) is that a single fixed payment will inevitably end up over-compensating some participants (specifically, those who actually participate very little) and under-compensating those who successfully adapt to the demand response model.

standards for providers, the utility could put in place transparent protocols that would allow entrepreneurs to fashion an array of demand response services to subscribing customers.

The Relationship between the State and the Market Maker

A well-tempered market for retail choice does not work by itself. The State and the state-regulated utility still have important roles to play, but those roles are different. In the utility of the future, the State and the utility-as-market-maker work together to provide two things that further customer liberation: ensuring that customers have the information they need to make commercial choices consistent with their preferences, and protecting customers against deceptive trade practices.

I explained in Chapter 2 why a free-for-all, laissez faire economy is not conducive to choice and runs counter to the public interest. Increasing the social good depends on the ability of each person to make—with confidence—a positive economic choice that increases satisfaction. The public interest does not depend on whether an individual in fact exercises that choice, only on whether social institutions afford any person the opportunity to do so. Making this public interest value real and practical depends on having institutions in place that make exercising these choices as easy as possible, without the danger that the institution might be corrupted from within by vested interests engaging in deceptive trade practices or manipulation. The public interest favors customer liberation, but for it to work, customer liberation needs a market maker.

The market maker must be clothed in both the perception and the fact of impartiality with respect to retail choice and competition. This means that it has no financial interest in any choice a customer might make. It also means that the cost of the market maker's operations is legitimately socialized, because the benefits provided by these services affect the characteristics of economic society.

141

Ideally, the market maker is not a judge or arbiter. Its natural functions are those of a clerk, although orders of magnitude more complicated. Arbitrating conflicts must rest elsewhere—with the State. While the market maker can use its mantle of impartiality to mediate disputes, conflicts that the disputing parties cannot themselves resolve need to be adjudicated by the entity that established the rules.

The Need for Information

The State and the market maker must cooperate to make sure that pertinent information is available to both retailers and customers. Metering customer usage will remain a natural monopoly function conducted by the retail market maker. It is a natural monopoly because having more than one independent entity competing to install meters leads to a higher level of market confusion, with the effect of increasing the cost of doing business in services where retail competition is natural.

Moreover, the ability of retail service providers to compete efficiently depends on "back office" protocols that do not impose extraordinary barriers to the ability of customers to switch providers. Among other things, this means that the data collected by the market maker on a customer's usage must be in a standard format. Any retail provider chosen by the customer should have full access to the customer's usage data as soon as the service agreement takes effect. If this data is in a standardized format, any service provider intending to compete in the market can test its information systems before opening its doors for business. Common back-office protocols established by the market maker help ensure one of the most important tenets of fair competition: nondiscriminatory market access.

Many markets in the United States that have moved towards greater retail customer choice have also instituted some standard requirements for product labeling. The label is a quick summary of the contractual agreement between the customer and the retail service provider that presents information on the features of a service plan that are most likely to be the customer's points of comparison and choice.

Such labels describe generally how the customer is billed (fixed rate per kilowatt-hour, a rate that varies by the time of use, rates that are indexed to wholesale prices, or rates that include a demand charge for the maximum level of usage during the billing cycle) and provide the average cost for a common level of consumption. Most labeling rules also require some disclosure about the fuel mix of the product's wholesale supplies. If a renewable portfolio standard is in effect for the service area, the fuel mix of the standard offering should be equal to the standard requirement.

Consumer Protection

The State and the market maker will also need to protect the consumer from snake-oil salesmen looking for any opportunity to scam a dollar. If the market maker is weak and state regulators are asleep, the opportunities will abound. There can never be any guarantee against fraud, but the State and the market maker can put measures in place that significantly reduce the opportunities for chicanery.

Existing laws already make defrauding customers a crime. However, one important component of prosecuting a criminal case is proving intent to defraud, and proving intent can be difficult in a new and complex arena of commercial activity such as the utility of the future. Many essential activities will be new, their need fully understood only by market participants, the market maker, and regulators who oversee the activities. It is unlikely that either the state regulator or the market maker will themselves have authority to prosecute criminal fraud, but they can set and monitor standards of behavior that, if violated, can substantially strengthen a fraud prosecution. The regulator, for example, can prescribe what a sales representative can and cannot promise during a call, or how a retail provider can verify that a service marketed as all-renewable actually comes from all renewable resources. The market maker can provide data on market operations to verify whether a participant is following rules and standards applicable to all other market participants. Prosecutors and courts tend to defer to the knowledge and expertise of regulators with respect to technical questions. If the regulator has established transparent and nondiscriminatory rules of behavior that can be substantiated by data collected by the market maker, intent to commit fraud will be easier to prove in court. More important, the knowledge that fraud has a high likelihood of criminal conviction will deter fraudulent practices.

One initial line of consumer protection is to establish eligibility requirements for companies entering the market. Requirements can include company executive's résumés, a list of the company's equity partners and primary lenders, and attestations that none of the principals has been convicted of or not are under investigation for a crime. Making this initial regulatory discourse public will give prospective customers a base of information they can use to research their options.

Another protection used in some markets is to require the posting of a surety bond as part of a company's certification as a retail provider. A bond provides up-front verification of a company's financial wherewithal. It also provides a ready source of cash for customer restitution if the company goes out of business and customers are left holding the bag.

Consumer confidence is an important pre-requisite for a well-functioning, robust market. The absence of strong and actionable protections against deceptive trade practices can have a chilling effect on consumer confidence. Striking the right balance is extremely difficult, however. Market rules define the economic playing field, inside of which market participants have the latitude to innovate. At the same time, getting the rules perfect the first time is next to impossible. Loopholes will arise, and the State needs to reserve to itself some flexibility to amend the rules as circumstances require.

Limits of Choice

The virtues of choice do have their bounds. This is where I depart from the libertarianism of economic purists. Choice is not synonymous with laissez faire; it need not be unlimited in order to serve both the public interest and the individual customer's interest. To put it more bluntly, customer liberation does not mean that society should be left defenseless against stupidity and greed. Reliability and a healthy natural environment continue to be shared public interest values under customer choice for electricity service. Options that impose a burden on the rest of society (by harming system reliability or causing excessive damage to the natural environment, for example) can legitimately carry an additional economic weight that disincentivizes them. Choices that would be socially pathological or that would maliciously harm others' ability to exercise choice can legitimately be kept off the list of options.

As a thought experiment, let's return to the example of electricity service provided 100% from renewable sources, where an RPS sets a minimum renewable content requirement (say, 30%) for the market. The basic choice for the customer is whether to take service with the generic 30% renewable content, or a service that sources from resources with a higher renewable content. Let's now add to the experiment a customer who hates the very idea of renewable energy, or who wants electricity entirely from coal, and is willing to pay more for it because of the damage it would do to the renewable energy market. This choice would increase carbon emissions and contribute to climate change, but from a market perspective that's not the worst consequence. Far worse is that such a product would compromise the ability of everyone else in the market to choose clean power. Rather than creating additional demand for renewable resources, the act of choosing clean energy would instead be making up for the customer who deliberately chose a product with a pollution profile higher than the social standard set by the RPS.

Reconciling such conflicts will be part of the State's new role in the utility of the future. The State might no longer define services and set prices, but it has an important role in deciding the public interest boundaries within which economic choices could occur. In our thought experiment, the public policy considerations would include the level of the generic renewable content requirement, the consistency of its application, and the integrity of the accounting system that would enable meaningful customer choice to occur beyond the minimum established by the RPS. These are fundamentally public-sector decisions which, once in place, provide a measure of market certainty around which private decisions can evolve.

Putting public interest boundaries around customer choice is not as contradictory as a laissez faire ideologue might argue. Any socioeconomic action has natural boundaries defined by what is technologically possible and by what is cost effective. Choice naturally comes with practical limits.

The notion of customer liberation as applied here to the utility of the future adds the public interest as an element defining the boundaries of economic possibilities. An individual will still seek a positive fulfillment of a desire for personal well-being within those bounds. Whether "well-being" means maximizing wealth, maximizing leisure, or maximizing flexibility to engage in pursuits that are personally rewarding in other ways, the field of economic choice allows for many options. Ruling out pathological choices is necessary to the public interest.

Case Study: The 1973-79 Oil Crises

Some history might provide a helpful set of reference points for customer liberation. One period in particular illustrates the differences in behavior between electricity customers who have the ability to respond to price signals and those who do not. The bookends of this period are the Arab Oil Embargo of 1973 and the Iranian Revolution of 1979. These two events marked the end of cheap oil in the world economy. While there are many lessons to be drawn from this period, here I focus on just a few that serve to illustrate price signals, electricity rate structures, and energy efficiency.

The beginning of the 1970s saw the collapse of international financial arrangements that pegged world currency values to gold. Middle East oil exporting countries responded by tying the value of oil to the U.S. dollar, but turbulence in the post-1971 currency markets still led to depressed oil prices. During this time, the Organization of Petroleum Exporting Countries (OPEC) coalesced from a loose-knit group of producing countries to a powerful international oil cartel. OPEC essentially had only one tool: the level of oil production from its member countries. But it was a powerful tool with tremendous international leverage. OPEC output constituted such a large share of global oil production that all oil prices responded with alacrity to any change in production orchestrated by OPEC.

Egypt and Syria invaded Israel in October 1973. Days after the United States began airlifting supplies to Israel, OPEC cut oil production and imposed an embargo on oil exports, causing global crude oil prices to quadruple within a few months. Oil prices stabilized at the higher level and stayed there for the next six years. Then a second oil shock hit world markets, this one caused by the Iranian Revolution in 1979. Market disruption was exacerbated even more when the United States froze Iranian assets in 1980 after militants seized the U.S. embassy in Tehran. The price of oil, which had never returned to pre-1973 levels after the embargo, again doubled in real dollars from 1978 to 1980.

During the ten years leading up to the 1973 oil embargo, the use of fuel oil in electric generation increased more than fivefold, so that by 1973 more than one-fifth of the country's electricity came from petroleum. The embargo slowed down growth in the use of fuel oil for two years, after which the trend resumed its upward trajectory up to the second oil shock in 1979-80.

The inflation rate during this time—itself largely driven by the response of crude oil prices to the international supply shortages—increased the price of nearly everything in the 1970s, reaching double-digit levels right after each of the two oil crises. The price of fuel increased faster than the general rate of inflation, leading to a commensurate increase in the cost of producing electricity. Recall from Chapter 3 the peculiar financial picture of the old-world utility under the regulatory contract: Fuel prices were simply operating costs that were passed through to the utility's captured customer base. This dulled the impact of fuel prices on the utilities themselves, because they were not picking up the tab. Consequently from 1973 to 1975, rates to end use customers rose 22% faster than the rate of inflation, with the single largest increase occurring in the months after the oil embargo. Inflation-adjusted electricity rates rose another 15% from 1979 to 1982 after the second oil shock.[50]

This is where we intersect the theme of customer liberation. The increase in retail electricity rates, which were still fully regulated by the State, constituted a massive price signal. Although it hit all parts of society the same, the responses to it differed. Because utilities themselves felt only a very dulled price signal, it took more than a decade for fuel oil to drop from one-fifth of the generation mix to less than 5%. The real story—actually, two different stories—played out with retail electricity customers, rather than with the utilities themselves.

---

[50]Higher oil prices had a different effect on utility net revenues, which in real dollars increased more than 20% during the two years leading up to the Arab Oil Embargo and then dropping by 8% from 1973 to 1974.

Parsing the Two Stories

Electricity today is both a classic factor of production and a factor of personal lifestyle. These are two fundamentally different modes of consumption, and they differ in how they respond to prices, uncertainty, and other economic forces. I begin, therefore, by splitting total demand for electricity between residential and nonresidential consumption. Untethering these two types of demand from one another makes it easier to see the causes and effects that drive the internal logic of each. It also reveals that the socioeconomic evolution of electrification has proceeded at different paces in the two stories.

Different things drive residential use and nonresidential use. Residential use is driven by what makes us humanly happy: community, culture, aspirations for our children, recreation, and all the various choices intended to bring us closer to a sense of personal satisfaction. A choice may be "rational" only in the context of a more complex logic where wealth is not the only source of personal fulfillment. Some might not be optimal or even "right" in the context of what the individual truly wants; the capacity for making life decisions is far from constant from one person to the next.

Nonresidential use—consumption for commercial activities and industrial production—on the other hand, is more legitimately measured by the traditional yardsticks of profit, savings, and economic efficiency. Cost and productivity are connected; the standard of new *tekhnología* is how it delivers benefit in the form of higher profits. The drivers are not psychological, but economic.

These two types of electricity consumption, shown in Figure 4 and Figure 5, are fundamentally different. Unfortunately, the most commonly used measures of electricity efficiency fail to distinguish between them. The two measures are electricity use per capita and electricity use per increment of real gross domestic product (GDP), sometimes referred to as "electricity

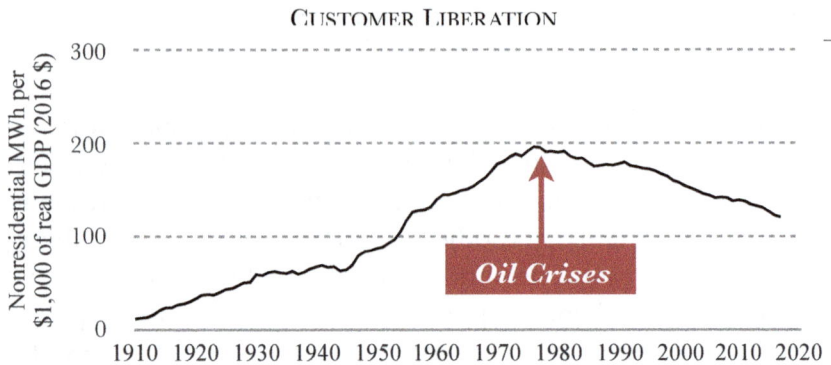

Figure 4: U.S. Non-residential efficiency (usage per dollar of GDP)

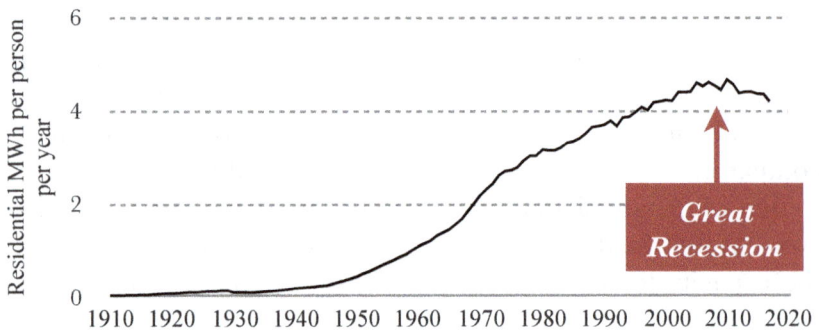

Figure 5: U.S. residential efficiency (annual usage per person)

intensity." They both aggregate (mistakenly, in my view) all types of consumption, thereby allowing trends in one story to be conflated with trends arising in the other. Therefore, I depart from convention and measure *residential* electricity use per capita, and *nonresidential* consumption using electricity intensity. This more accurately distinguishes the two as functions of lifestyle and economic production, respectively.

More importantly, my alternative approach tells with more clarity and greater accuracy the two different economic stories of how creative destruction is playing out in the evolving power sector and how customers are adapting to the new opportunities. We see two turning points: a clear shift in the economic productivity of nonresidential electricity use beginning with the oil crises (which hardly fazed residential efficiency), and what could turn out to be a corresponding shift toward efficiency in residential use after the Great Recession.

The Efficiency Story: Nonresidential Electricity Use by U.S. Businesses

Nonresidential consumption—electricity used mostly for industrial production and commercial activity—is relatively easy to understand economically because it fits nicely into the production function and all the related quantitative trappings of neoclassical economics. Labor and capital are the fundamental factors of production, of course, but it is technology that determines how efficiently the two combine to produce profit for the firm and economic well-being for society. As *tekhnología*, this includes not only gadgets such as computers and internet servers but also social organization, operational protocols, capital investment, and even government regulation.

Electrification began sowing the seeds of creative destruction throughout the economy even before the Great Depression. By World War II, the United States had already achieved a certain level of electrification, which increased slightly under the adaptations required in a wartime economy. After the war, electricity use per dollar of real GDP accelerated due in no small part to a post-war economic expansion led by increased consumer purchasing, especially for automobiles and durable goods.

Thus by 1973 the U.S. economy had completed more than half a century of electrification in manufacturing, services, and most other sectors of the productive economy. Natural obsolescence provided built-in opportunities in many sectors for reducing costs by substituting inefficient old processes with newer ones that were more efficient. By the time the oil embargo sent the first major energy shock throughout the U.S. economy, electricity use had matured to the point that many businesses could explore process substitutions that could help maintain their levels of production with less electricity.

One factor that helped many businesses achieve such substitutions was the structure of electricity rates. A commercial business such as a bank or an insurance company uses electricity differently than an industrial operation such as a steel mill or oil refinery. The voltages needed to keep an office running are substantially smaller than the voltages needed to refine steel. The business hours of an office are also different from a large-scale manufacturing process. These differences in usage patterns place different stresses on the infrastructure needed to deliver electricity, and can affect the utility's need for new capital investment.

Nonresidential rate structures have taken different customer usage patterns into account for a long time. At the time of the oil shocks, nonresidential had for years been billed based on a combination of energy and demand. "Energy" refers to the total volume of kilowatt-hours delivered to the customer over the course of the billing cycle. "Demand" refers to the highest amount of power (measured in kilowatts) that the customer takes from the grid at any moment during the billing cycle. Thus, for an operation consuming a large amount of power only a few times per month, demand might constitute the largest portion of the company's monthly electric bill. For an office with consistent but low-level use, energy might be the largest part of the bill.

The sharp and persistent pivot in nonresidential electricity use per dollar of real GDP after the oil crises therefore indicates long-term behavioral changes in the direction of greater production efficiency induced by higher energy prices. The productive capacity of the economy had matured to the point that a significant number of businesses could switch to substitute processes that used less electricity. The ability of these substitutions to become cost reductions was enabled to some degree by the structure of the rates charged by the utility. Of course, they could save by using fewer kilowatt-hours during the month, but they could save even more if they used electricity in a way that flattened out surges in monthly use.

The Happiness Story: Residential Electricity Use in U.S. Lifestyles

Residential consumption is more challenging theoretically. Only by an extreme stretch of reasoning can the nonlinear forces that affect residential consumption be stuffed into the square hole of what drives economic productivity. The economic choices of individual human beings have many inputs that are not rational in a pure economic sense, because they are expressions of personality: fashionable or frumpy; high-tech or Luddite; junk food or organic; simple or ostentatious; couch potato or outdoorsy.

It was not until after World War II that electricity began to grow as a component of individual lifestyle.[51] Thus at the same time nonresidential demand was entering a period of maturation after the war, households were just beginning to learn what electricity could mean for personal lifestyle. By the early 1970s, this meant central air conditioning, electric stoves and heating where natural gas connections were not available, and more food storage using stand-alone home freezers.

Unlike business consumption, the level of electricity use in the residential sector demonstrated little response either to the effects of the Arab Oil Embargo or to the second oil supply

---

[51] To put it numerically, nonresidential consumption during the war was only 200 kilowatt-hours per person per year—roughly equivalent to the energy it takes today to run a laptop computer for a year.

shock in 1979-80.[52] Consumption of electricity per capita continued to increase despite the inflationary pressures caused by higher oil prices. Some of this continued increase was due to continued customer expansion; more people were becoming residential electricity customers. But even after accounting for this broader change, residential electricity consumption per person continued to increase after 1973, indicating continued changes in society towards more electricity-intensive lifestyles—unabated by the rising costs.

The fact that residential use per person did not respond significantly to higher energy prices suggests that, at that juncture in the country's socioeconomic evolution, electricity demand was price-inelastic. In other words, the types of uses that made up the growth in residential demand in the 1970s tended to be essential rather than discretionary. If one lived in a newly built all-electric home, substitutions for cooking were limited. If a family in the South installed air conditioning to make the long, hot summers more livable, turning them off might increase health risks to the elderly.

Another factor contributing to the residential sector's lack of response to an economy-wide price signal is that the form of residential rates did little to reward energy-efficient behavior. Unlike business customers, residential customers only had energy charges. This limited the options for modifying behavior except by reducing the total amount of electricity used. There was no

---

[52] There are two ways to measure lifestyle efficiency: per capita and per residential customer. The former measures total residential use against U.S. Census population estimates; the latter uses the number of residences to which the utility sends bills. Thus, the utility might send a bill to one residential customer at an address where four people live. A major factor driving the increase in per-capita electricity use is that more households (and therefore more people) were becoming electricity customers. The number of residential electricity customers per population increased steadily throughout the 1960s, but continued to increase at a similar pace in the 1970s during the oil embargoes. The trends I describe in this section are borne out similarly regardless of which measure is used.

reward for running dishwashers and electric dryers at night, and no incentive to avoid running refrigerators and air conditioners during peak load. Thus, not only did residential customers have little flexibility for making substitutions, they had no rate mechanisms available to them to help them save money even if they managed to do so.

Continue the story line up to the Great Recession of 2008 and 2009. Recent data show what could be the first steps in a persistent trend towards declining electricity use per capita (although too few years have passed between the recession and the writing of this book to call it an unambiguous trend). What is clear, however, is that

- electricity is a much bigger part of personal lifestyle in the 21st Century than it was in the 1970s, moving beyond inelastic essentials to encompass personal computing, entertainment, and other more discretionary forms of consumption
- choices for substitution are prolific (this is evident from comparing EnergyStar appliances to models that are less energy efficient)
- customers in many areas are beginning to have choices for alternative rate plans

Rolling these conditions into a bundle, one can hypothesize that the typical individual in 2008 was in a better position to respond defensively to a severe economic downturn than was the case in 1973. And as happened among business customers in the 1970s, some of these recession-induced changes in behavior might stick. So far, this is exactly what appears to be happening. The post-Recession period from 2010 to 2016 has seen a continuous decline in the amount of electricity consumed by the average person, something that has never happened in the history of U.S. electricity service. While this bears monitoring into the future, one very plausible hypothesis is that this trend is yet another consequence of creative destruction, this one manifesting on the demand side of the equation. If so, it adds empirical weight to the need to redefine the public interest and to update the regulatory contract.

Conclusion

Perhaps the least useful approach to understanding the utility of the future's retail effects is to assume customers will flock to new technological possibilities just because they're there. They won't—not unless these new shiny things result in some tangible value that reduces the customers' bills or better meets other customer preferences. Failure to understand the very complex relationship between creative destruction and customer liberation could end up with an unintended (and perhaps unconscious) attachment to one of the vestiges of the old-world utility: assuming that customers passively react to what the utility offers them. Not only does that insult the customer's intelligence, it fundamentally misses how creative destruction is changing the retail side.

Customer liberation will demand flexibility of the future utility. Its retail-facing operations will need to cater to the most discriminating customers, fully understanding that not all customers will be as picky. Some (but not all) will be ready to squeeze every dollar of value from price signals; some (but not all) will be willing to adapt their usage patterns to accommodate clean energy. The utility's challenge—especially with respect to the operation of its distribution system—will be to accommodate a wide range of preferences in the most economically efficient manner.

The future utility will also need to be flexible with respect to entrepreneurs. Unleashing value may require a level of creativity and risk-taking that have never been part of an electric utility's cultural DNA. Rather than learn new tricks, it may be more effective for the utility to enable entrepreneurs to compete with one another in some of the service areas traditionally provided by the utility itself.

The Great Recession of the late 2000s could usher in a permanent change in lifestyle choices similar to the change triggered by the oil crises of the 1970s in consumption of electricity in economic production. The tribulations of the time forced many to look harder at lifestyle efficiency. If combined with more choices for retail electricity service, these experiences could lead to a social trend towards greater efficiency in residential electricity use—which the utility of the future should encourage.

Chapter 6: Updating the Regulatory Contract

The old approach to regulation won't work for the utility of the future. Market structures can be too dynamic to wait for a docketed case with plaintiffs, intervenors, and clearly delineated questions for litigation. The State's job in this new paradigm will be on-going monitoring and maintenance—the care and sustenance of a healthy, living market. It will require anticipating potential problems and getting ahead of them by pro-actively eliminating loopholes that allow predatory behavior. The State will therefore need sufficient flexibility to take creative action.

Much of the State's part of the new regulatory contract necessarily falls with regulatory authorities. It relies greatly on deference to the regulator's technical expertise, but that carries an implicit expectation that the regulatory authorities acquire new skill sets. As a result, many states, along with the Federal Energy Regulatory Commission, now rely more heavily on "informational" dockets and other fact-gathering proceedings to build up-to-date knowledge to guide their proceedings.

Deference aside, however, much of what regulators can do is bounded by state utility codes. Some of the new responsibilities might fall within a regulatory agency's existing statutory authority, but some might not. Therefore, this chapter is also written with governors and state legislators in mind. Implementing a smooth transition to the utility of the future could require coordination among the executive and legislative branches of government to ensure that every element of the transition can withstand judicial challenge by older entrenched interests that stand to lose a historical position of advantage.

Some of the State's historical public interest functions (deciding questions involving eminent domain, for example) will of course continue. The State will also continue cost-of-service regulation for parts of the electricity sector that remain natural monopolies. Transmission and distribution assets will still be public infrastructure, and their cost will need to be allocated in a manner that is fair to society. But the scope of this type of regulation will be narrowed to those functions that are still natural monopolies. Generation and retail sales will be in a new market environment, and this will require a new approach to regulation.

Misconceptions abound about how the utility of the future is to be regulated—or not regulated—so the first task in this chapter is to distinguish fact from fiction. The State's responsibilities under the new regulatory contract correspond to the two new public interest focus areas described in this book: competition and customer choice.

The Myth of Deregulation

Few terms in the electricity business have been as misunderstood and misused in recent years as "deregulation." One can almost use it as a litmus test: the more a speaker uses the term as shorthand for the changes that have taken place, the more they reveal how little they really understand what is going on. Worse, the word subtly diverts the conversation away from the real transformations taking place.

The most extensive electric sector reforms in the United States have occurred in Texas. It is instructive that the word "deregulation" never occurs in any form anywhere in the 52,000-word state law adopted in 1999 that set electric sector restructuring in motion. By contrast, the word "competition" occurs in some form more than 170 times. The phrase "customer choice" occurs more than 100 times and has its own separate section in the law. Thus, instead of "deregulating," the law redefines with legal exactitude the new regulatory contract between the State and the essential components of the electricity sector in a market environment that has been restructured for competition and customer choice.

160

Deregulation is not where the public interest lies. The Texas law framed the public interest within the combined framework of customer choice and competition. Retooling of regulatory institutions supported these two public interest objectives, which were new priorities for electricity service.[53] Texas unbundled the traditional investor-owned utilities into three pieces: a generation company (which for convenience I will refer to as a "genco"), a retail electric provider ("retailer"), and a wires company consisting of the transmission and distribution assets.[54] Power generation and retail service were opened to competition. Except for temporary controls imposed on the spinoffs of the former bundled utilities, competitors in the genco and retailer spaces could set their own prices and terms of service.

The *technical* capability to fragment the electricity supply chain and dispense with the need for monopoly is never itself a guarantee of competition. Things can go wrong, and the State's new regulatory role is to make sure they don't. In this new world, "regulation" brings into its competency the role of monitoring market conditions to ensure that competition is healthy, open

---

[53] The law begins by stating its premise for all that follows: "The legislature finds that the production and sale of electricity is not a monopoly warranting regulation of rates, operations, and services and that the public interest in competitive electric markets requires that, except for transmission and distribution services and for the recovery of stranded costs, electric services and their prices should be determined by customer choices and the normal forces of competition."

[54] Unbundling could be actual—separation of the utility into three new and independently owned companies—or it could be functional, in which the operations remained as three operating subsidiaries of the same holding company. One of the regulatory agency's first tasks in Texas restructuring was to establish a detailed code of conduct governing how three subsidiaries could interact with one another. Putting these codes of conduct in place involved major regulatory proceedings, because the stakes for the whole restructuring effort depended so much on them. Over a short period of time, however, each of the utilities divested their regulated transmission and distribution operations into independent companies with their own boards, stockholders, and capitalization.

and fair, and that the business practices used by retailers to compete for customers are not deceptive.

Many of the issues that arise in this new market environment involve judgement calls that cannot be left to self-interested market participants with varying degrees of influence and knowledge. A spike in wholesale market prices, for example, is a flag that something *might* be wrong, but is not in and of itself positive proof that the market has failed. Recall that a market-based economic framework depends on price signals to encourage and discourage behavior, especially new investment. Price signals can legitimately go up, as well as down, depending on how the fundamentals of supply and demand intersect. Still, the legitimacy of a run-up in prices will naturally be viewed differently by those who pay them and those who benefit from them.

The State's new role is to be the fair social arbiter of when high prices are legitimate price signals and when they are not. If the price hike is not legitimate, the State also has the responsibility to decide how to correct the matter in a way that does not entail further unintended complications. So instead of regulating specific business decisions such a pricing, the State regulates the economic environment in which market participants make such specific decisions themselves based on their own reading of price signals. The State's new regulatory objectives concern the integrity of price signals, establishing market rules that are transparent and nondiscriminatory, detecting and preventing the abuse of market power, ensuring that retail customers have the information they need to make informed economic choices, and cracking down on any individual market participant that deliberately aims to deceive customers or manipulate the market.

These new regulatory functions are in many ways harder than the traditional functions, which to a large extent were detailed accounting tasks. Adding up numbers and dividing the result among customer classes is one thing. Investigating behaviors that are not specifically addressed in market rules and deciding whether they constitute market manipulation is a different matter, because it often requires a State authority (the regulator, or the court if the regulator's decision is appealed) to make a subjective yet legally binding determination about the applicability of a broadly written rule to a specific circumstance. For the electricity sector, it is a new application of the rule of law. The market itself cannot do this.

The notion that any electricity market has been "deregulated," therefore, is nonsense. Regulation continues, even if it doesn't resemble what it looked like in the past. The utility of the future requires a rewriting of the regulatory contract that requires the State to take on new responsibilities, a revision made necessary by the new convergence of technology, economics, and consumer preferences.

Mitigating the Threat of Market Power

Competition is one of the public interest pillars on which the utility of the future rests. Nevertheless, competition can be perverted if the rules governing it are not fair, effective, and enforced. Instead of channeling entrepreneurial effort toward creating new value, the market can easily degenerate into competition to secure unproductive rents—leeching wealth out of the economy without returning any new value. The State is all that stands between healthy competition that benefits society and the chaos of profligate rent-seeking.

The exercise of market power is the oldest and most systematic way to extract rent from the economy. Market power, when boiled down to its essence, occurs when one single market participant (or a handful of them acting in collusion) is large enough and dominant enough to control prices. It might choose to raise prices and boost its revenues, or it might use its power to strategically suppress prices for a while to drive smaller competitors out of the market.

A mathematical heuristic used to quantify this capability is a *pivotal supplier test*; it involves subtracting the largest supplier from the total supply pool and then comparing the remaining supply to demand. If residual supply is not enough to meet demand, the largest supplier is said to be pivotal. As novelist Mario Puzo's Don Corleone might have described it, a pivotal supplier is in a position to make the market an offer it can't refuse.

In all organized markets, market prices are set by the unit with the highest offer price among all the least-cost offers selected. Imagine all offers arranged on a supply curve in order from least expensive to most expensive based on offer price. If demand is 90,000 MW, security-constrained economic dispatch moves up the curve to the point where the cumulative supply equals 90,000 MW. The supplier that offers the 90,000th MW selected (call it Generator A) is the *marginal* generator. The offer price that Generator A places on the 90,000th MW that is selected sets the payment price for all other offers that are selected. Except for Generator A's offer, the offer price of all other supply that is selected is lower than that offered by Generator A. For each selected offer, the difference between the *market clearing price* (the price of the marginal megawatt offered by Generator A) and its offer price constitutes its *inframarginal profit*.[55]

An unrestrained pivotal supplier can control prices in two ways. Because it is pivotal, some part of its supply will always be selected regardless of how the rest of the supply curve is priced; the market cannot clear without some part of the pivotal entity's

---

[55] This is how market clearing prices form if there is no transmission congestion on the system. If, on the other hand, dispatching the generators with the lowest marginal costs would overload one or more lines, SCED adjusts the dispatch. It reduces generation from the units contributing to line congestion, and replaces it with an equal amount of power from more expensive units on lines where there would be no congestion. Each point on the system then has its own marginal price, based on how much one additional MW of demand at that point would increase total generation costs. This essentially remakes each node on the grid as a nested sub-market within the larger market.

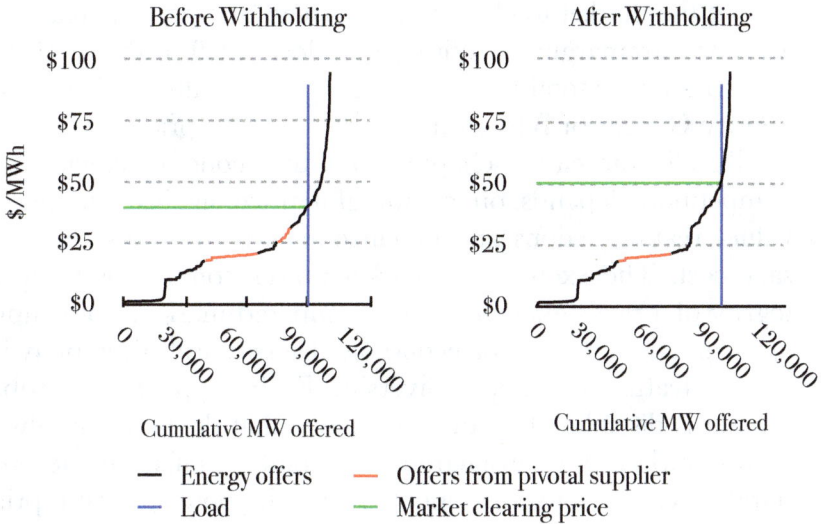

Figure 6: Illustration of how a pivotal supplier can affect prices

supply. Thus, the pivotal supplier can command any price it wishes on its supply without running the risk that it will price itself out of the market.

The pivotal supplier can also withhold some of its generation from the market, thereby effectively shrinking the total supply pool. Assume, for example, that the pivotal supplier has a large block of generation with a marginal cost of $20 per MWh and a smaller block at $30 per MWh. It prices each amount at its marginal cost, which for both blocks is below the $40 per MWh offer of Generator A who would normally be on the margin. If the pivotal supplier keeps its $20 block in place but takes its smaller block off the market, the total supply in the market effectively shrinks. Generator A is no longer on the margin; now Generator B is, at $50 per MWh. Generator A is still in the money, but now has an inframarginal profit of $10.

The pivotal supplier technically left some money on the table when it took its smaller block off the market. But because it

165

caused the market to clear at $50 instead of $40, it increased by $10 the inframarginal profit on the block it left in the market. It reaped a larger total profit by causing the smaller and more expensive Generator B to set the market clearing price.

Recall from earlier chapters how the economic efficiency of competition depends on meaningful price signals that reward value-creating actions and penalize actions that cause unnecessary cost. The exercise of market power compromises the integrity of price signals. In a well-tempered market, both supply and demand are pools of economic diversity. Substitutability is a crucial feature of supply diversity. Each supplier in a robust market is disciplined by the knowledge that demand can always turn elsewhere for satisfaction. A pivotal supplier, on the other hand, need not be so assiduous. It has the power to raise prices without adding any new value into the market.

The draconian remedy for market power is divestiture—breaking the pivotal supplier into independent smaller firms that are not pivotal. A less drastic and more common remedy is to constrain what the pivotal supplier is allowed to do in the market. Behavioral mitigation requires the pivotal supplier to act the same way any other market participant would: offer all its available supply into the market at its marginal cost of production. A marginal cost offer means that the supplier will not generate power if the additional cost of generation (mainly fuel and other costs that vary with the amount of electricity produced) is more than the market clearing price but will if the price is above its cost of production.

The State faces a number of challenges in controlling market power, however. For one thing, there is a difference between simply having market power and abusing market power. A pivotal supplier might have market power, but if it is offering all of what it has into the market at the true marginal cost of those resources, State authorities will be hard pressed to prove that price signals have been distorted.

There is very little useful precedent to guide those regulating the future utility for market power, and what precedent is available is mostly borrowed from economic sectors that did not start out as utilities. Thus, the traditional tools and precedents of antitrust law do not entirely address the market power issues that could arise with the utility of the future.

Antitrust commonly focuses on mergers. Its concern is whether the combined company has persistent market power in its industry, as measured by customer subscriptions, annual unit sales, or similar indicators that are either static or that change very slowly. A common metric used generally in antitrust is the Herfindahl–Hirschman Index (HHI), which provides an index of market concentration based on these static indicators. The HHI can be calculated using pre-merger market shares, then recalculated combining the shares of the companies planning to merge. If the merger causes the market's overall HHI score to exceed a threshold, it can raise anticompetitive concerns and trigger additional investigation as to whether the merger would harm customers.[56]

Contrast this somewhat static HHI metric with pivotal supplier measures used in a number of RTOs. Being pivotal in an energy market that is run every five minutes can be very dynamic. In a real-time market with five-minute dispatch, a pivotal supplier test would need to be calculated 105,120 times per year —and that does not include measurements of the day-ahead energy market or auctions for the procurement of reliability-based ancillary service capacity. Having a pivotal supplier in just a few of those time periods would be less of a competitive concern

---

[56] The HHI is calculated from competitor market shares measured in percentage points. Each competitor's market share is squared, and the results across the entire market are summed. U.S. Department of Justice guidelines are that a market is considered highly concentrated if the HHI is greater than 2,500. Thus, a merger that would cause an HHI below 2,500 to increase to more than 2,500 could trigger a higher level of scrutiny for market power concerns.

than having a supplier who was pivotal during most of them. Determining when to be concerned and how to interpret the metrics are subjective calls made by the regulator, and traditional antitrust law provides no useful benchmarks.

One other danger exists apart from the threat of market power abuse: the threat of market manipulation. This is somewhat different, however, because the perpetrator can be a smaller market participant that technically does not have a large share of the market.

Market protocols in an RTO are necessarily complicated. This is to ensure that actions taken by the market maker are not arbitrary, and that the rules governing each action the market maker takes are formulated in a transparent manner. For example, RTOs require a generator to perform according to its schedule or as instructed by the RTO, and to do so within a reasonable band of deviation. This is easier for a controllable generator such as a combined cycle natural gas plant, however, than it is for a generator that uses wind or solar power. Thus, stakeholders might agree to different deviation provisions for renewable resources that are significantly less controllable than thermal generators.

However, problems can arise with respect to payments and penalties that are linked to a generator's deviations and the schedules on which they are calculated. If any payments (compensation for operator-ordered curtailment, for example) are tied to the generator's schedule and the penalties for schedule deviations are waived, the wind or solar generator has an incentive to overschedule its anticipated output above what the forecasts say about that period's probable wind or sunshine. If the grid operator needs to order curtailments to avoid a reliability problem, an inflated schedule could result in higher curtailment payments because it would appear that the generator reduced generation more than it actually did.

Some of the most egregious and devastating examples of market manipulation occurred in California's early restructured market in 2000 and 2001. Enron Corp. was not the largest generation owner, but it had schooled itself on the intricacies of California's market rules and the opportunities that lay hidden in them. Among its strategies were

- wheeling power between California and price-regulated markets and profiting from the price differences;
- creating the appearance of transmission congestion in the day-ahead market, and then changing its real-time dispatch to get paid for solving the congestion it had artificially created; and
- strategically withholding capacity from the market to drive up prices.

This type of behavior, while not necessarily done by a supplier with market power, nevertheless constitutes the type of malignant rent-seeking described in Chapter 4. It takes wealth out of the economy without returning anything of value. This is one of the most difficult puzzles for the regulator, because the rent-seeking behavior does not involve the violation of any rules implemented by the market maker. Closing loopholes in the rules is the most effective remedy, but it is never possible to anticipate all the possible loopholes.

Nevertheless, the ability of competition to achieve the public interest aim of greater economic benefit depends on the containment of malignant rent-seeking activity. Even if it is a regulatory game of cat-and-mouse, it is something the State needs to do. Furthermore, it is something *only* the State can do, because the market maker lacks the enforcement power. Market participants themselves certainly cannot be left to self-police, because each one has a microeconomic incentive to manipulate the market if it can get away with it.

Because of all these factors, the regulator has a delicate balance to strike. Market participants—those waiting for an opportunity to get away with mischief as well as those competing honestly and in good faith—need to know with a high degree of confidence that the State will prosecute manipulation and market power abuse. At the same time, the regulator's interventions cannot be so heavy-handed as to stifle normal competitive behavior. There is no clear formula for where to draw the line.

Consumer Protection

Just as the State must protect market participants, it must also protect customers. The State cannot protect all customers from all hazard, and it cannot protect customers from their own poor judgment. But if the market is to work for society at large —which it must if the public interest is to be served—conditions must be such that customers exercising a reasonable degree of caution can find the service they want with minimal chance of fraud.

The new regulatory contract tasks the State with four main roles on the electricity sector's retail side:

- setting rigorous and nondiscriminatory standards for companies seeking to enter the market as retail service providers;
- making sure customers have the information they need to exercise choices that are consistent with their preferences;
- cracking down on fraud and deceptive trade practices so that retail customers have confidence their economic choices will be honored; and
- ensuring an orderly flow of information between the customer, utility, and retailer—including safeguards to ensure cybersecurity.

Standards for Market Entry

The first function of regulation in a competitive retail context is setting standards for market entry. Confidence is the psychological oil of a well-tuned market, and confidence depends significantly on having highly-qualified competitors. While they do not preferentially decide who gets to compete, regulators do have the task of setting certification standards applicable to any provider. Certification might include a requirement to post a surety bond with the State, with the proceeds to be used to mitigate harm to customers in the case of unexpected bankruptcy, illegal behavior, or other circumstances that cause the provider to abandon the market suddenly.

The key aspect of certification standards is that they are nondiscriminatory—equally applicable to any company seeking to enter the market. The aim is to screen out "fly-by-night" enterprises who have a high risk of failing to honor their promises to customers, and to screen them out before they have a chance to harm customers. Strict standards with non-trivial bonding requirements discipline market entrants to have a convincing business plan.

Arming Customers with Information

Customer choice means little if customers don't know what their choices are. In many areas where customer choice has expanded, regulators have developed standard terms of service and disclosures that all retailers must provide to their customers. These standards include explanations of charges, length of contract, cancellation provisions, and other points of information that clarify what the customer is signing up for.

State authorities can also develop marketplace tools that help customers narrow down their preferences. One tool used in several markets is a "facts label" similar to the nutritional label found on most packaged foods. A facts label for electricity service includes basic information for a specific plan, presented in a standard format that makes side-by-side comparisons easy. Information can include the type of charge (fixed or time-of-use, for example), the effective cost (in cents per kilowatt-hour, or as a

171

monthly total for a typical user), the percentage of supply for the product obtained from renewable energy resources, and the minimum contract period.

If there are many providers and many types of service, the State can also provide a web-based shopping platform that combines fact labels for all products into a searchable database. For example, a customer who wants all-renewable service can filter all available plans to a smaller number that only includes green power. From there, the customer can compare rates on different types of green power plans.

The information provided through the state platform is essentially a cataloguing exercise, carefully designed for thoroughness and impartiality. But it is not innovation—that remains with the entrepreneurs competing in the marketplace. Credibility and confidence depend on the information platform being managed by someone who has no vested interest in which providers succeed and which ones fail. Because the need for objective integrity arises from the public interest (as differentiated from the private interest of a provider) the job of building this common information platform necessarily falls to some arm of the State—be it the regulator, a consumer agency, or a contractor hired by an agency.

Cracking Down on Fraud

Malice can wreck even the best-intentioned policies in the best-designed market. Fraud undermines confidence in the market, especially if it is not prosecuted vigorously and visibly. It compromises the public interest value of customer choice and the full liberation of consumer preferences. Consumers may settle for less than what they really want, not because of a rational choice but because they are afraid of being cheated.

Policing against fraud has been the State's job in other parts of the economy for a long time, but it is new to retail electric competition. Being under the regulatory microscope, a monopoly utility did not have even the structural opportunity to engage in consumer fraud. Service could be terrible, leading to a surge in complaints to be arbitrated by the regulator. But that isn't a felony like deliberate fraud.

Because fraud is a crime, protecting society against it requires the State to use a heavier hand than is required by normal regulatory functions. A full-forced prosecution often requires the State to prove that the defendant acted with an intent to defraud. This can be difficult if the State's regulatory arm has not promulgated standards of behavior guiding how retailers interact with customers. If such rules are in place, however, proving intent involves fewer evidentiary hurdles. Thus, the prosecution of fraud involves coordinated efforts by the State's regulatory arm and its police arm in the form of the agencies that investigate and prosecute corporate crimes.

A similar regulatory role is the prevention of predatory customer engagement practices. The regulator can establish rules that prescribe how a competitive provider may and may not contact prospective customers, such as do-not-call lists and prohibitions against unauthorized switching. Unlike preventing outright fraud, the prevention of predatory practices aims to reduce practices that make it inconvenient for customers to exercise their economic choices.

One common predatory practice is "slamming," by which a retailer switches a customer from another retailer to itself without the customer's permission. Slamming can occur when authentication standards are lax or can be circumvented.

Predatory practices can also include overly aggressive marketing by telephone or in person at the customer's door. When taken to the extreme, this type of predatory practice can limit a customer's ability to compare options and arrive at a rational economic decision. Both choice and competition are compromised.

The Flow of Commercially and Personally Sensitive Data

Another new responsibility that falls to the State is the protection of customer data. The new economic environment of the future utility brings several issues regarding information into conflict. Privacy has always been a concern, but a new issue given the transformations taking place in the sector is that the realization of value depends on associating behaviors with price signals. This necessarily involves more exchange of data between the customer and the utility, the utility and the customer's retailer, and the customer and the retailer. This means that if a customer prefers greater choice, that customer's privacy will have to be safeguarded carefully.

Even if the customer opts for greater choice and is comfortable sharing information with the retailer, the problem of data security remains. Widespread data hacks in 2016 relied on internet-enabled devices other than computers. As more commercial data flows between the customer, distribution utility, and retailer, the need for constantly updated security protocols only increases.

All these functions—establishing market entry requirements, disseminating information to consumers, prosecuting fraud, and ensuring proper use of customer data—necessarily fall to the State. They are essential to the creation of an orderly commercial environment in which consumer preferences can be effectively and efficiently satisfied. Even though this type of market-enabling activity is a major change from the State's old role of setting rates for the monopoly utility, it is nevertheless essential to the public interest.

The Regulator and the Market Maker

The State and the market maker have a special partnership when it comes to defending the market against fraud and manipulation. While the market maker cannot itself wield the State's police power when it sees suspicious behavior, it can provide regulators with important market intelligence and expertise.

The wholesale market maker is the clearinghouse for all data moving through the mechanisms that determine prices and dispatch. Moreover, much of this information is competitively sensitive, which means that the only entities who normally see it are the market maker (who is obliged to protect the data) and the market participant itself. If the State's investigation into market power abuse or manipulation requires a forensic analysis of the data, the market maker is a natural partner. Just as a coroner and a detective work together to piece together the facts to determine whether a death was an accident or a homicide, State investigators and the market maker examine offers, outage schedules, and generator performance to determine whether there has been any systematic effort to distort market outcomes.

All RTOs operating in the United States have an independent market monitor keeping track of wholesale competitiveness. The market monitor is usually unaffiliated with the RTO and is not answerable to it. Nevertheless, it has full access to RTO data and thus can reconstruct in full any operating interval where the market outcome might be suspicious. In addition to investigating potential manipulation and market power abuse, the market monitor provides periodic assessments of how well the competitive markets are working and will often flag rules and procedures that systematically lead to inefficient market outcomes.

Both the market maker and the market monitor are technicians with high-level expertise in economics, operations research, and technical modeling. They are at an arm's length from the official prosecutorial power of the state, but they can assist in the forensic investigation and can provide disinterested expert testimony on market outcomes and the esoteric processes leading up to them. The regulator, market maker, and market monitor together are the economic cops walking the beat of the wholesale and retail marketplaces to ensure that everyone is playing by the rules.

Conclusion

Regulation in this new market environment, then, focuses on market conditions rather than price setting. The goal is to ascertain whether the market can work well enough to produce outcomes that are at least as good as—and preferably less costly than—what would result from conventional cost-of-service regulation.

Among the questions that regulatory processes address are:

- Does any competitor have the ability, either unilaterally or acting in collusion with others, to control prices or prevent new competitors from entering the market?
- Is there enough transparency in market operations for a competitor to manage risk and prepare for reasonably foreseeable contingencies that could affect supply or demand?
- Can market rules be manipulated or gamed to prevent economically efficient outcomes or to secure unjust economic rents to the company manipulating the market?
- What public interest issues outside the realm of electric sector market operations are affected by market outcomes, and how can they be accommodated in a way that does not compromise the ability of the market to provide economically efficient outcomes?

Regulation, therefore, does not go away. Rather, the State's role evolves into something more complex and more vital to the efficacy of the future utility. Regulation involves gauging the ability of a market to sustain competition and ensuring customer choice. The State, through its various public interest mechanisms, also has the job of determining the extent to which its markets can sustain competition and crafting the transition to restructuring as it is feasible.

Chapter 7: The Electric Utility of the Future

Now we can consider the future electric utility itself. The preceding chapters have set the stage. The two engines of social change shaping this transformation are the evolving public interest and the economic process of creative destruction. These two forces combine to produce two complementary socioeconomic effects: On the supply side, the dissolution of natural monopoly and the emergence of competition; and on the demand side, a diversifying field of consumer preference with respect to electric service.

These forces will take on different institutional guises in different regions. The ability to sustain competition is a crucial factor that determines how quickly and how deeply monopolies dissolve and choice becomes robust. So, while the evolutionary drivers behind the utility of the future are universal, the speed at which they unfold is not. Some markets might quickly support robust competition, while other markets might not. Competitive responses will differ, thus the form of the future utility at any given point in the future will necessarily vary.

Revisited: What is a Utility?

Let's begin by returning to the concept of "utility." Up to this point, my use of the word has been somewhat imprecise. This has been for convenience. The business of creating and delivering electricity comprises many activities that, at least up to recent years, have been recognizably bundled within one organization. Most everyone is accustomed to calling this organization an electric utility. Even federal and state laws apply a rather broad-brush definition to the term. Federal law, for example, says an electric utility company is "any company that owns or operates facilities used for the generation, transmission, or distribution of electric energy for sale."[57] That is a huge tent, but it served well enough for most of the sector's commercial history. All the activities that could fit into this expansive definition had enough real "utility-ness" about them that it made sense to regulate the whole bundle through a single entity.

Creative destruction is changing the foundations of these activities from something old into something new. The term "electric utility" has been a convenient way to describe the "something old" part of this socioeconomic process. As I've discussed throughout this book, however, some of these previously bundled activities are losing their inherent utility-ness as they transform into "something new." The public interests bound up in them are changing. Habit is a poor reason to keep things bundled together when they are in fact losing their fundamental similarities, so no such bundling is assumed in this chapter. Consequently, for the remainder of this book, "utility" is strictly applied to activities that come out of the crucible of creative destruction with an enduring public interest that justifies monopoly treatment. Some activities that have historically been part of the "generation, transmission, or distribution of electric energy for sale" will not fall within this definition. At the same time, new functions will be encompassed by the term. These market-making functions will tend to expand our idea of what a utility does.

Where explanation involves a reference to what is falling away, I add "incumbent" as a modifier to the term. The "incumbent utility" is the corporate organization as it used to exist before creative destruction.

Ironically, applying a more exact definition of "utility" results in a less exact picture of whether a given entity is truly a utility. All "utility-ish" functions could be bundled into the same regulated entity, or they could be split into separate companies. For many reasons, the set of functions that remain bundled into

---

[57] 42 U.S. Code §16451

a *bona fide* utility will not necessarily be the same from one region to the next.

A utility, as discussed in this chapter, means an enterprise that combines into its organizational purview *only* those activities that remain either natural or virtual monopolies, or that are needed from a ministerial perspective to sustain healthy competition. Utility activities interface with non-utility services and activities provided by competitive entrepreneurs. But while one competitive provider can be replaced by another with little impact on the overall delivery of electricity, the utility (and the State-franchised functions that remain exclusively in its wheelhouse) is irreplaceable. The ability of competitors to participate in the market depends on the supporting services provided by the utility. Therefore, if competition in these non-utility activities is in the public interest, the utility has a social responsibility to ensure competition operates efficiently and fairly.

Distribution functions—the infrastructure that transforms power from the wide-area bulk energy system to lower voltage levels and delivers it to end-use customers—largely remain with the utility. Following the examples of restructuring already accomplished in New York and Texas, we may refer to these activities as being provided by a *distribution utility*. A distribution utility's utility-ness arises primarily from the public inconvenience of having more than one set of substations, feeder lines, and usage meters physically encroaching on a neighborhood's public and private spaces.

The Full Model: Structural Unbundling

In this fully matured model, finding something that even looks like a traditional incumbent utility is about as difficult as finding a rotary telephone on a spaceship. Dealing with one lugubriously responsive entity is replaced by a dynamic panoply of competition.

A customer's choices shape what the future utility looks like for that person. Simplicity is always an option, but it carries a cost. Imaginary Harry, for example, has many things occupying his mind that have a higher priority than his electric bill. For him, the best choice was an electricity service plan with one simple rate that is in effect all the time. A renewable energy standard sets a social minimum for clean energy content; Harry was content with that. He felt no drive to do anything more.

Harry could choose from among dozens of retail service providers who had a simple fixed-rate offering. The prices might have varied because each provider has a unique set of cost considerations—none of which Harry saw or cared to see. For him, the choice was simple: Pick the provider offering the lowest fixed rate locked in for the longest time. Because the market was so competitive, however, all simple-service providers tended to converge on the same price. For Harry, the tie-breaker was to compare customer service ratings, which led him to choose Basic Service Company.

Next door, Ideal Lucille is a different sort of customer. Her mother used to clip grocery coupons religiously. Today Lucille is an energy saver. Her household appliances and lights are energy efficient, and all can be tied into a home energy management system. After evaluating a handful of bids from installers and selecting the one whose financing plan best fit her budget, she also installed solar panels on her roof.

Lucille then shopped for a contractor to set up her home energy management system. The one she chose linked her appliances, solar panels, and the battery on her electric car with the advanced electric meter the distribution utility had on her house. The contractor then gave Lucille the link to his company's web app and showed her how to simulate different time-of-use rate plans. After trying out different schedules for using her appliances and charging her car, she selected a plan.

Finally, Lucille shopped to find the retail electricity service provider who offered the type of service she wanted at the lowest mark-up over wholesale prices and using all renewable energy. She signed on with Custom Service Company. The plan Lucille chose tracks the grid's cost of producing electricity hour by hour. If bulk electricity delivered from the grid to her neighborhood is cheaper at 1 p.m. than it is at noon, the electricity she uses at 1 p.m. will cost her less than what she uses at noon. Custom Service also included a special demand-side incentive with Lucille's plan: Anything she uses between midnight and 6 a.m. (when her electric car is charging) is free. And because her home energy management system keeps major appliances from all coming on at the same time, her ability to avoid spikes in her usage saves Lucille even more money. She has calculated that her savings are large enough that, over a short time, she will cover the fee she paid to the energy services contractor, as well as her other efficiency-related costs.

Just as her mother made every penny count, Lucille takes advantage of even the smallest price incentives offered by her retail service provider and the distribution utility. Her solar panels earn her an additional credit because the advanced inverters linking the panels to the grid help the utility maintain reliability for the whole neighborhood. Lucille's home energy management system tracks real-time prices against her electricity service plan and how she uses electricity. The system's monthly report tells her how much more she could have saved with further adjustments to her usage patterns. If the adjustment is reasonably simple and the potential savings appear to be consistent, she can modify the settings on her management system.

Even when Lucille uses the same amount of electricity Harry does, her bills are less than his because she uses it at times when her service provider's supply cost is low and her provider's plan passes those savings on to her. But because her appliances are more energy efficient, Lucille does the same things Harry does but with less electricity, reducing her bills even more.

The difference between what Harry pays and what Lucille pays is Harry's convenience premium, which he will choose to keep paying if there are other things in his life that are more important for him to spend time on. Most significant, Harry's preference for convenience in no way conflicts with Lucille's preference for efficiency and renewable energy sources. The utility of the future accommodates both—along with a host of variations in between them.

Behind the Outlet and Beyond

Despite their differences, there is one very important similarity between Lucille and Harry. Both have very little interaction with Neighborhood Distribution Utility, the monopoly that owns the hardware to move electricity from the regional grid to each customer in town. They see the meters on their homes and the power lines that crisscross their neighborhood. They both see on their monthly bills the same line item for charges related to the general service provided by Neighborhood Distribution. But despite their many other choices, neither Lucille nor Harry actually chose that utility. It is a natural monopoly that serves everybody. The utility provides its meter data to the retail service providers Lucille and Harry have chosen, but primarily the two customers deal with their providers, not the utility.

To provide Lucille, Harry, and everyone else with innovative product choices, the utility must give retail service companies full access to the usage data coming from the customers' meters. More detailed information enables providers to tailor plans to fit customer preferences. For example, if Neighborhood Distribution only lets retail service providers know how many kilowatt-hours their customers use during a billing month, the only point on which providers can "compete" is price per kilowatt-hour. They will have no ability to translate detailed price signals into more refined plans that can save customers more money on their bills, because they will not have the information necessary to connect usage patterns with price signals.

Harry, Lucille, and the rest of the neighborhood will see the Neighborhood Distribution's service vehicles when extreme weather takes down a feeder line and blacks out the neighborhood. The lines remain monopoly-owned assets that are clothed with a public interest, and for this reason the cost of building and maintaining them is socialized across every customer on the distribution system. If economic growth is bringing more people and more businesses to the area, it is the distribution utility that conducts the analysis needed to plan what new feeder lines and substations might be needed. It is the distribution utility that estimates the cost of all these essential services and argues the need for every dollar before the State. These separately counted distribution charges are assessed to every customer regardless of who their provider is.

Neighborhood Distribution is one of several distribution utilities each serving its own area and connecting to the regional transmission grid, RTO Interconnection. RTO is largely invisible to Harry and Lucille (except when things go seriously wrong). It acts as the central utility managing the use of the high-voltage network connecting a diverse pool of generation companies (gencos) with a diverse pool of retail service providers, each of which serves a diverse set of customers. Custom Service and Basic Service deal with the RTO on behalf of Lucille, Harry, and all their other customers.

RTO's market dispatch procedures determine wholesale power costs for each specific point on the grid. The neighborhood where Harry and Lucille live is one of those points, and the wholesale price of power there can change every five minutes depending on the intensity of neighborhood load and conditions elsewhere on the grid. This localized time series of prices is what Basic Service and Custom Service each pay to the RTO for the electricity it sells to its customers in the neighborhood, based on how much electricity their customers use at each hour of the day.

Like retail sales, electricity production is also competitive. The primary venue for competition among gencos is RTO's security-constrained economic dispatch (SCED). Every genco submits a separate offer for service from each unit it has on RTO's network. If it wants to maximize its likelihood of being used and paid, the genco submits its lowest feasible offer price at each point on the network it can provide power. RTO runs SCED for every market interval, determining what the least-cost bundle of generation is based on demand and setting the price at which each selected unit is paid. The point-specific prices coming out of SCED determine how much a generator gets paid at each point, and how much a retail service provider pays for the electricity it delivers to its retail customers at each point.

Like the distribution utility, no one competes with RTO and RTO does not compete in any of the contestable markets that it manages on its system. With respect to information about the transmission system, all roads lead to RTO: schedules for the next day's demand; forecasts for wind power production; generators or transmission lines that are scheduled to be out of service for planned maintenance; reserves available for reliability management; and critically, the instantaneous value of electricity generated or used at all points on the grid.

The retail provider Basic Service is indifferent to where its electrons come from, so long as the cost is as low as possible. It pays the localized price coming out of SCED for Harry's neighborhood and focuses on reducing costs in other parts of its operation. One place it has not scrimped, however, is wholesale price forecasting and risk management. Basic Service has been reasonably on target in projecting regional fuel costs, total demand, and other factors that influence wholesale prices in the places it serves customers. It has used these forecasts to determine the best pricing terms for the service it provides to Harry and other customers who prefer the convenience of a simple electric bill.

Like all other retail service providers in the market, Basic Service has a minimum renewable energy content requirement. It satisfies this requirement through simple market exchanges using renewable energy certificates (RECs), which represent metered, generator-specific, time-stamped electricity produced from a renewable energy facility. Renewable power and RECs that have not been otherwise sold to a specific buyer are offered on the open market to providers, such as Basic Service, that do not focus on green power but nevertheless have a minimum renewable content requirement.

Custom Service caters to a more discriminating customer base. Unlike Basic Service, Custom Service negotiates power purchase agreements with specific gencos based on what Custom Service has committed to provide to its customers. The company has developed daily demand profiles for various types of customers—including those like Lucille who own an electric car, want 100% renewable power, and can adjust their consumption patterns in response to price signals. Custom Service matches the daily load profiles with the daily generation profiles of wind and solar power in the region. Custom Service has supply agreements with Genco Wind and Genco Solar, in amounts and schedules tailored to the combined load profiles of its customers. To reduce its exposure to wind and solar variability, Custom Service has also procured capacity from Genco Geothermal for a round-the-clock baseload quantity of power.

Gas Genco is one of many conventional power generation companies competing in the RTO's market. It has a number of natural gas fired combined cycle plants and combustion turbine plants. Like its competitors, Gas Genco secures fuel for its conventional thermal generators separately using a strategic combination of long-term contracts and short-term purchases. Whether its most efficient combined cycle plant, Ace Generating

185

Station, can make money in the market depends on the balance between what it costs to generate a megawatt-hour and the price that clears the market at the generator's point of interconnection. Gas Genco sets Ace's offer price based primarily on two factors: the efficiency with which the plant can convert natural gas into electricity and the cost of natural gas based on the company's fuel procurement strategy.

Because Ace Generating Station is a new and highly efficient plant, wholesale power prices cleared by the RTO tended to drop everywhere—including the point serving Lucille and Harry's neighborhood—once Gas Genco brought it online. Gas Genco normally offers Ace into the market at a price well below what clears through SCED, and the margin between clearing prices and Ace's actual operating cost contributes to Gas Genco's ability to support its equity and long-term debt requirements. So even though Ace Generation Station's entry into the market caused prices to fall generally, it still made money.

Wind Genco and Solar Genco have a different strategy for pricing their generation in the RTO market. They have no fuel cost, so their marginal cost of generation is near zero. Their strategy is to offer all they can generate into the market as price takers: the offer price is zero, which mathematically means they will accept any non-zero price that clears the market in each SCED run. Some of their renewable plants are under contract with retailers like Custom Service, but a few are more speculative. Where clearing prices tend to be high and resources are good, the newest and lower-cost technologies allow the gencos to bet on the market.

Gas Genco, Solar Genco, Wind Genco, and Geothermal Genco all compete in the same market on the same economic basis through SCED. One characteristic they share is that they are all merchant generators. All their capital costs come from various combinations of long-term debt financing and equity shares. The gencos' banks and equity partners shoulder all the risk of capital recovery, which in turn depends on the market prices that clear the RTO's dispatch auctions. None of them has a guaranteed backstop for cost recovery.

The Partial Model

In the world described in the previous section, everything about the utility of the future comes together without friction. Perfection is not a prerequisite for progress, however. Structural factors might make competition problematic in one part of the sector or another, but that is not an obstacle to letting market forces work where they can.

There also may be factors outside electricity operations that depend on keeping retail service a monopoly franchise. If a significant share of a city's operating budget comes from its municipally-owned utility enterprise, the city's fiscal stability might depend on maintaining the utility as a revenue-generating monopoly. In the restructured Texas market, for example, municipally-owned utilities were exempted from the requirement to open their service territories to retail competition, although they became stakeholders and competitors in the wholesale market. Their generating plants are dispatched on an economic basis by the RTO along with all other generators on the system.

Forcing competition or customer choice onto a market when the conditions are not yet ripe will cause more harm than good. Many of the conditions that define the utility of the future evolve along independent tracks, and at different speeds. The way to the future utility might not be a total quantum leap from one paradigm to another for the entire supply chain. It could instead be a glide path where each transitional step is guided by the opportunities at hand.

Either generation or the retail sales might need to remain a monopoly franchise in a transitional model. The basic question is whether that part of the business can sustain genuine competition. More specific questions include:

- Does any participant have market power?
- Are there any other unreasonable barriers to a new competitor entering the market?
- Is the supply market flush with legacy assets that still have significant economic life in them?
- Is demand too thin to sustain competition that is robust enough to allow a start-up to manage its risk of new investment?

Answers to these questions are necessary to developing a political consensus about whether competitive conditions are sufficient to sustain the further liberation of customer preferences.

Retail Competition and Customer Choice[58]

A diverse customer base within a large utility service area might sustain customer choice even if the wholesale market lacks enough breadth to sustain robust competition among generators.

---

[58] Community choice aggregation (CCA) is one type of transitional model. I distinguish it from a retail choice transitional model, because from the customer's perspective it generally replaces monopoly with duopoly. This is a very modest improvement with respect to encouraging competition among retail suppliers. The CCA model involves a local authority (often a city government or a specially created local utility district) procuring wholesale power and selling it to subscribing customers. For example, if voters in a city pass a referendum to authorize community choice aggregation, residents would eventually have the option to continue taking service from the incumbent utility that still serves the remainder of the region, or switching service to a new retail entity created by the local government. Even if all eligible residents switch, the incumbent utility would continue to own and operate the distribution system, transmission system, and its fleet of generators—much the same as the transitional model described above. The incumbent utility would take on the role of providing infrastructure and reliability services that enable the retailer (in this case, the aggregator) to serve customers. It would also be the default retail provider, serving those who do not choose to switch to the aggregator. The community aggregator, as an entity created under the authority of the local government, caters to local preferences for electricity service that are different from what the incumbent utility provides. This often involves renewable energy goals that are more aggressive than state standards. It is still a closed retail market, however, because no other competitive supplier may enter the market. The local franchise protects two retail providers rather than one.

The array of individual commercial preferences might vary too much and too strongly for the utility to serve efficiently. In this type of market, the incumbent utility would shift roles from supplier to market maker. Independent competitive retail companies would deal with customers directly, while the utility would maintain the distribution network and provide information services.

What Harry and Lucille see when they make their different electricity-related decisions in this partial-model world is much the same as in the full restructuring model. The differences occur largely on the other side of their electric meters. The distribution, transmission, and generation functions are still under the organizational umbrella of the traditional incumbent utility. The difference is that, as a matter of policy clearly established by the State, the utility integrates these functions in a somewhat different way with the added goal of facilitating retail competition. It becomes an expanded market maker, with supply management being part of the market-making role.

One fundamental change for the utility is that it is prohibited from competing for retail customers. While it still maintains the neighborhood distribution system, operates the grid, owns generation, and purchases wholesale power, it can no longer receive money from customers for anything other than the cost of distribution services. This is because the incumbent utility's historically protected and exclusive relationship with all retail customers in its service area would give it enormous market power if it were able to compete.

The utility could remain as a provider of last resort to which a customer would temporarily default in the event a competitive retailer went out of business, or if for some reason the customer was dropped from normal service. This would still be a highly regulated retail service, however. Because it would embed extraordinary costs related to providing short-term contingency service on a moment's notice, it would necessarily be more expensive and less flexible than what a customer could obtain from any other competitive provider. "Choosing" the provider of last resort, in fact, would be an economic oxymoron.

In this intermediate model, the State establishes entry requirements for competitive retail providers just as in the full restructuring model. It also monitors competitive conditions in the retail market, provides consumer education and support tools to make choice easier, and prosecutes cases of fraud and deceptive trade practices. This part of the revised regulatory contract is essentially the same as it is in the full restructuring model.

Start-up costs for Custom Service Company, Basic Service Company, and all other retail service buyers clubs competing for business in this new market are also similar. If they have access to the same customer usage data they do in the fully restructured markets they serve, these providers can test creative product offerings that have proven successful in other markets.

As the market maker, the traditional utility's distribution operations manage the flow of customer usage information between the customer and the customer's retail provider. The data is detailed enough that the retailer can customize charges by time of use and intensity of demand, as well as the conventional metric of total kilowatt-hours consumed during the billing period.

The conventional utility is still regulated with respect to generation. It still owns power plants—in fact, the size of its legacy generator fleet could be one factor slowing down the transition to wholesale competition. Being a virtual monopoly keeps it under State scrutiny, but the nature of regulation changes.

The State's goals are twofold. First, the State must determine how to balance competing financial priorities affecting the incumbent utility's legacy generation fleet. These are plants whose capital costs are being recovered through the utility's rate base, giving them a significant economic advantage over merchant generators. The State needs to decide how to balance two considerations: the enjoyment of benefits by the public from investments the public is already paying for and reducing the tendency of these legacy assets to inhibit the development of merchant generation.

The issue posed by the size of the incumbent utility's legacy generation fleet is the problem of stranded assets. Walking away from long-term obligations and agreements made under the old regulatory contract would compromise the public interest by undermining the State's own creditworthiness, just as defaulting on a loan would hurt any private individual's credit score. It is therefore left to the State to balance the use of legacy assets with the need to procure new resources consistent with new customer demand.[59]

The State's second goal is to ensure competitive retailers can, if they choose, procure energy supplies from merchant generators without undue interference by the incumbent utility. This would involve protocols for the use of the incumbent utility's transmission system. A competitive retailer might, for example, offer a number of all-renewable services to customers. The utility itself could enter into supply contracts with new wind and solar developers and earmark those sources for the competitive retailer. Alternatively, the retailer could enter into its own bilateral agreements. In this case, the utility would provide delivery service via its transmission system under the provisions of its transmission tariff. Either way, the State's regulatory objectives are to ensure that the incumbent utility is fairly paid for the service it provides to the retailer, to ensure retail competition is not being suppressed by the utility's supply practices, and to ensure that no

---

[59] The restructuring effort in Texas addressed these legacy assets through a special short-term customer charge. In essence, this charge represented the outstanding cost of investment that would have been recovered through the old bundled utilities' rates if the monopolies had continued. The restructuring law authorized the regulator to conduct a special proceeding to determine the value of such "stranded" capital costs, and to put them into a special charge that was universal and non-bypassable until the remaining costs were fully recovered.

practice by the utility unduly favors one retail competitor over another.

As the dominant supplier and transmission owner, the utility also takes on the job of day-ahead scheduling, ancillary service procurement, and real-time dispatch. These functions need to culminate in a settlement process that accounts for all commercially relevant aspects of energy delivery to each retail provider. For example, if a provider has a number of customers signed up for all-renewable service, the daily settlement needs to have accounting mechanisms that authenticate an exclusive, verifiable match between supply and demand.[60]

Conclusion

To borrow a phrase from psychologist Carl Rogers, the utility of the future is a direction, not a destination. The vision I have attempted to lay out in this book addresses the forces behind the sea changes that are happening in the electric sector. These social and economic currents are strong, I believe, but they do not carry all boats to one and only one port. The scenarios described in this chapter are merely a compass. The roadmap is up to policy makers and the utilities under their jurisdiction.

The aim of this chapter is to provide down-to-earth descriptions of what the utility of the future might look like. I say *might*, because the details of this illustration are far less important than the economic and public interest phenomena behind them. Competition and customer choice are the powerful socioeconomic phenomena that are pushing *tekhnología* along this evolutionary path. They are the watchwords for the future utility,

---

[60] As I explained in Chapter 5, the accounting used to match supply and demand within a pool of electricity flows does not mean electrons from a specific wind or solar plant flow exclusively to a specific electric outlet. If properly designed and implemented, a system of renewable energy credits can provide a low-cost and transparent means for authenticating the delivery of renewable power to retail customers.

but by no means are their forms limited to this chapter's illustration.

While important directions for the future, competition and customer choice are also a compass for opportunities in the electricity sector today. One can take any region's electricity market as it stands right now and test it against these values. It is basically a matter of asking which direction for change feels more natural: Towards competition or towards monopoly? Towards greater customer choice or towards less? As energy sector analysis evolves along with the sector itself, these intuitive tests can be reinforced by empirical study.

One grid characteristic should be evident in this chapter's illustrations. Competition and choice require more flexibility throughout the entire supply chain. As a result, the utility of the future is an adverse economic environment for gigaplants. One massive plant would absorb a large amount of the sector's productive capital and lock it into a single asset. This would mean less responsiveness to changing economic conditions and less resilience if something were to happen to that one huge asset. Spreading productive capital across a portfolio of assets that are smaller in size but greater in number provides an added measure of flexibility for both operational contingencies and retail demand that is more diverse and dynamic.

Creative destruction works through price signals. This book has examined price signals from different perspectives: capital formation, operational efficiency, and retail choice. Any technological innovation in any part of the supply chain will enter the market with an associated price signal, and its ultimate impact on the future utility will depend on how this signal meshes with everything else affecting competition and choice. One of the new opportunities that price signals enable is the entire field of demand response—end-use customers providing grid services that once could come only from power plants. Information technology is enabling demand response; prices signal when and how much the grid needs.

Many uncertainties lie on the path between today's electric utility and the utility of the future. Still, evidence suggests it is a worthwhile path to take and enough information exists to discern the way forward.

Afterword

December 2017

The electricity sector has continued to evolve during the two years it has taken to write this book. The changes over this small span of time have been consistent with the socioeconomic forces I have described. Even the reactionary pushback against new *tekhnología* that Schumpeter anticipated as inevitable resistance to creative destruction seems to have intensified. The course of evolution continues nevertheless: the foundations of utility monopoly continue to fracture, and customers continue to demand more from their electricity providers.

This afterword puts the theoretical discussion of the preceding chapters in the context of two matters that have been especially challenging to public- and private-sector decision makers throughout the electricity sector:

- the controversy surrounding net metering for rooftop solar, and
- the diminishing role of baseload generation.

These two issues highlight the tension between creative destruction's strong evolutionary momentum and the stubborn refusal to look at the world differently. They have been discussed by many others, and it is not my aim to repeat what they have already argued. What will be more useful, I believe, is to look at them in the context of creative destruction, the new public interest, and the changes to the electricity sector that have been discussed in the preceding pages. With these new lenses, I hope to introduce a new perspective to the discussion that could help policy makers and regulators find a working consensus on institutional changes. The industry itself will continue to change; that is inevitable. The trauma of that change, however, is not.

Strategic policies can help workers, investors, businesses, and customers weather the changes constructively.

Net Metering for Rooftop Solar: Price Signals, Part 4

Net metering is one of the most unusual and ironic tensions between the old-world monopoly utility model and the utility of the future. Caught in the middle is distributed photovoltaics (PV), or rooftop solar. While rooftop solar interests, regulators, policy makers, and other special interests have often clashed over net metering policies, they have also been accidental co-conspirators in resisting the tide of the electricity sector's evolution. Despite their other differences, all sides often limit their vision to outcomes that will fit neatly into the box of convention, postponing action on the sector's larger socioeconomic growing pains. Indeed, this mutual resistance to real evolutionary change often results in net metering—which is a terrible fit with the future paradigm—being the least-terrible option left on the table.

Net metering was one of the first tools for accommodating rooftop solar. The panels and inverters connect to the fuse box on the customer's side of the meter, and the power they generate reduces the amount of power drawn from the network. By switching to two-way mode, the meter can track excess power flowing back to the distribution network. When the customer's usage is less than the power generated by the PV system, the excess power causes the meter to run backwards. Thus, the meter readings from one billing period to the next represents the net of kilowatt-hours used by the customer and kilowatt-hours generated by the photovoltaic system. If the net usage for the month is zero, the customer pays zero. If it is negative, the customer builds up a credit.

In this way, net metering pays for energy from rooftop solar at the same constant cents per kilowatt-hour rate used by the utility to charge for electricity. However, this simple rate structure is itself a lazy, low-technology convenience carried over from the old utility paradigm. It fosters inequity and cross-subsidization to a degree that increases every day as customer usage patterns become more diverse. (Chapter 5 explains why and how.) Net metering is by no means the only problem with simple rates; it just makes a bad mechanism worse.

The net metering problem is limited to residential customers because their rates consist almost entirely of a simple, cents per kilowatt-hour charge.[61] Let's call this simple structure "dumb rates," in contrast with "smart rates" like time-of-use pricing, demand-sensitive charges, demand response plans, and other billing methods that reward customers for cost-saving behaviors. Dumb rates suppress nearly all behavioral price signals to residential customers, regardless of whether they have rooftop solar or not. It doesn't matter, for example, whether the customer runs heavy appliances in the evening when the utility's cost of procuring power is high, or after midnight when the cost of power is low. The dumb rate charges the same for each kilowatt-hour regardless of when it is used.

Residential customers who tend to use electricity in ways that are efficient (thus reducing the utility's cost of service) end up subsidizing those who are less efficient. The dumb rate averages out the differences with the simplifying assumption that all customers use electricity in pretty much the same way—even though they don't.

Rooftop solar adds a new twist, but trying to address this piece of the problem while leaving all other sources of cross-subsidization untouched is discriminatory. It is also futile, because a simple piecemeal solution carries a high risk of unintentionally creating new problems (the regulatory "whack-a-mole" dilemma).

---

[61] Industrial customers and large commercial customers are billed differently, and these rate structures already respond to cost-causing behaviors related to surges in use and maximum levels of power demand. This reduces the tendency for cross-subsidization with respect to transmission and other fixed infrastructure.

Moreover, the dumb rate used in net metering has nothing to do with the value of rooftop solar. For residential customers, it represents all the costs associated with producing and delivering service reliably—not only the cost of producing energy, but also the cost of maintaining reliability, recovering from natural disasters, and doing ordinary business such as payroll and taxes. Regulators review and adjudicate all of these costs in the utility's rate case, with the total revenue requirement allocated to all classes of customers through their base rates.

Rooftop solar has value that can be measured and quantified, but that value does not enter into calculating the dumb rate. It is here that rooftop solar interests often fall back on a simplifying assumption of their own: that all of the benefits of rooftop solar magically equal the value of the dumb rate. The cost of service per kilowatt-hour becomes the value of solar energy per kilowatt-hour based on the untested assumption that everything will work out in the end.

With net metering, end-use customers with rooftop solar panels drift indiscriminately between being an energy producer and an energy consumer. This has given rise to the economically nonsensical term "prosumer," which seems to suggest that simultaneously being a producer and a consumer is new and special to rooftop solar. But it really isn't. Every employee engaged in the production of goods or services anywhere in the economy goes home at the end of the work day and consumes other goods and services. *Homo oeconomicus* has always been both a producer and consumer.

If anything, net metering's special effect is to muddle the individual's rights and responsibility in both roles. Normally, prudent individuals involved in a commercial transaction of any type protect their interests by clarifying the terms of the deal. Terms of employment specify the worker's rights and responsibilities as a producer of goods or services. When that same individual takes off the producer hat and puts on the consumer hat, the task of defining rights and responsibilities begins again in a new context. This is true whether one is buying a car, deciding on a warranty plan for a new computer, or even comparing food labels in the grocery store. Net metering largely skips over the need to fully define rights and responsibilities for an individual customer and the utility in the specific context of the new value provided to society.

As bad as net metering might be, the only way to get rid of it in a manner consistent with the sector's new public interest principles—choice, competition, and rates based on cost causation— is through broader rate reform that distinguishes between production and consumption, treating each role on its own merits. The basic elements of the path forward include the following.

- Keep the customer's role as an energy *producer* separate from the role of energy *consumer* in every way (separate metering, separate accounting, separate pricing, separate terms of service).

- Pay the customer for energy based on the value of energy, not the rate charged for delivering service. Ideally the payment price should vary with supply and demand conditions throughout the entire wholesale market. If not, it should be set in its own regulatory proceeding.

- Charge the customer for electricity service (regardless of whether they have rooftop solar) using rates that are based on cost causation, distinguishing the cost of energy from the cost of reliability and other non-energy costs.

- Remove all unreasonable barriers to the ability of customers to aggregate under a qualified third-party service provider.

The keystone is rate reform for everyone. Charges for electricity service should separate the cost of energy from all other costs of providing electricity service. Any costs charged per kilowatt-hour should be limited to the commodity cost of energy and should vary with changes in the wholesale commodity price of electricity. Infrastructure costs—particularly the cost of transmission, substations, and distribution lines—ideally should be charged based on how much the customer contributes to the need for these fixed investments through efficient or inefficient use. Most of this can be captured through a demand charge that is based on the customer's maximum load (in kilowatts) at the time of the utility's system peak demand. For average customers, these reforms would tend to result in final monthly bills that are little different from what they would have been with dumb rates. Efficient customers would see lower bills, inefficient customers higher.

The formula used to pay for solar should include bonuses for system features that add value, such as battery storage and inverter capabilities that help the distribution utility maintain reliability. Payment should be time-sensitive so that it increases or decreases along with hourly and sub-hourly changes in the price of wholesale electricity. It should also be location-sensitive, paying more where rooftop solar reduces other local costs of service.

With a rate structure tied to cost causation in greater detail, the customer can then choose whether to apply rooftop solar generation as an offset to consumption or as paid production—but not both. Incorporating battery storage can help arbitrage value between both choices, allowing stored solar energy to smooth out momentary peaks in usage (electric water heating, for example) or to feed into the grid when prices are favorable. The key is to structure rates for *all* customers in a way that provides meaningful price signals, rewarding behaviors that save energy and reduce the cost of keeping the grid reliable.

Value increases with scale, so policy should enable third-party energy management companies to aggregate many customers into a single generator group. The aggregator would be a single point of interface with the distribution utility and would manage telemetry between itself and all of its subscribers. This would

200

simplify matters for the customer with rooftop solar; in exchange, payment would depend on whether the customer's usage patterns help or hinder the aggregator's ability to respond to operational instructions from the distribution utility. The customer could choose among providers, or choose a "lone wolf" approach and deal with the utility directly.

If the State decides they are warranted, additional incentives can be added to the rooftop solar payment formula, with the costs recovered from all energy-consuming customers. Socializing the cost of the subsidy based on the four principles described here means that those who themselves have rooftop solar and receive the subsidy would also pay their share of the subsidy.

Ultimately, the path to maximum deployment of rooftop solar passes through an evolutionary landscape. Evolution is not selective; one cannot ride the tide of creative destruction when it is profitable and expect to jump off when some benefits flow in a different direction. Radical rate reforms might initially involve some pain for rooftop solar, but fighting the change (rather than adapting to it with the development of new business models) is a short-term tactic that will ultimately leave the industry worse off.

Sunset for Baseload

Next, we turn to the loss of baseload generating capacity. Especially among coal and nuclear advocates, the assertion is that having less baseload capacity will lead to less reliability, less resilience, and a potential grid disaster.

It won't. Here's why.

A system's "base load" is the minimum amount of customer demand during a typical 24-hour period. The logic of baseload operation is that if one generator were to produce at the base load level (or at a constant proportion of it), the grid would need

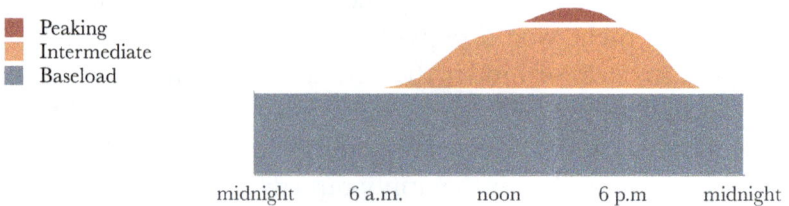

Peaking
Intermediate
Baseload

midnight   6 a.m.   noon   6 p.m   midnight

Figure 7: Baseload generators in a monopoly utility's daily operation plan

no change in the plant's output over a long time.[62] Historically, the task of matching generation to load in real time was a three-point triage (illustrated in Figure 7): round-the-clock constant operation of a few large generators; turning intermediate load-following generators on in the morning and turning them off at night; and filling in the remaining gaps between total demand and total generation with peaking units and interruptible load.

Baseload was a convenient and cost-effective way to manage the largest piece of generation when information moved by telephone and data resided on floppy disks. That is not today's grid, however. Nearly every generator connected to the grid has a supervisory control and data acquisition system that is in constant communication with the grid control center. This allows operational information and instructions to travel back and forth much faster than they ever could at the beginning of the giga-plant building spree, and in vastly larger volumes. Moreover, every bulk power system with large amounts of variable renewable resources, such as wind and solar, uses short-term forecast-

---

[62] One way to sort through the confusing terminology is to distinguish between "base load" (two words) as a characteristic of *load* and "baseload" (one word) as a way of operating *generation*. Base load refers to the hour-by-hour shape of total demand during a typical day. Baseload refers to special operational attributes of certain generating units. There is no absolute linkage between base load and baseload generation, apart from the etymological link.

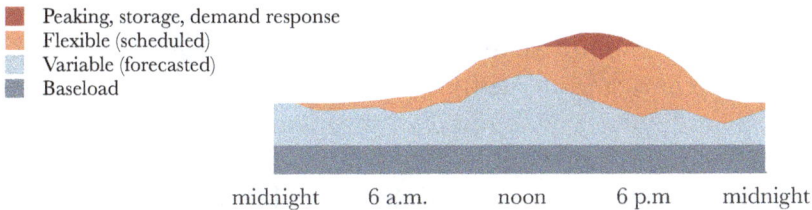

Peaking, storage, demand response
Flexible (scheduled)
Variable (forecasted)
Baseload

midnight   6 a.m.   noon   6 p.m   midnight

Figure 8: Example of daily operation profile with grid modernization

ing to estimate how these generators will perform the next day.[63] Interruptible load has also evolved into more sophisticated, orderly, and varied options for demand response that have greatly expanded the types of load that can participate in the market as virtual generators. Add to this the emerging role of large-scale batteries and other forms of energy storage that can provide even more responsiveness. The grid is flexible, and it is smart enough to use that flexibility to achieve many objectives cost effectively.

With all the computational power available to the modern utility, planning for the next day no longer needs to be reduced to be three simple slabs of time layered on top of one another as illustrated in Figure 7. Indeed, doing it that old way ends up costing customers more money. The system optimizes each hour as an integrated whole. The daily minimum demand level—the original "base load"—is almost irrelevant.

The modern grid can still accommodate baseload generators, as illustrated in Figure 8, but the operational convenience

---

[63] Research and experience have shown that a wind or solar forecast need not be perfect to be useful. The forecast guides operators in deciding how to schedule generators such as natural gas units that are both controllable and operationally flexible. With the right amount of reserves on line, any difference between projected and actual wind production can be accommodated along with the normal momentary deviations in customer demand. Studies have shown that the additional benefit of having a perfect forecast compared to state-of-the-art forecasting is minimal, due to how operators use the forecasting in planning their day-ahead schedules.

203

provided by these plants no longer has the enormous and irreplaceable premium value it had four decades ago. Flexibility is now the characteristic with premium value, and baseload plants —coal and nuclear—do not offer flexibility.

Baseload generators have other operational characteristics that are unrelated to base load demand. These include the ability to store fuel on-site and relatively low outage rates. But it is important to remember that while these attributes help grid resilience, they never guaranteed it in the past and might not be the best options in the future.

For example, extreme freezing conditions are a recurring challenge to regional grid reliability. These events have caused forced outages even at coal plants, which are vulnerable to many of the same on-site issues that can affect plants fueled by natural gas: sensor failure, ice in steam delivery lines, and other problems caused by operating at temperatures below what the plant's design can accommodate. Looking solely at fuel supply issues, however, both coal and natural gas alike have vulnerabilities. The list of potential issues for coal includes on-site piles of fuel frozen solid, and failure of the conveyor system. For natural gas, the supply challenges during a freeze event can be physical (much less gas delivered into the pipeline system, accompanied by much more home heating demand) or contractual (caused by the generator procuring too little fuel ahead of time and not being able to find more on the intra-day spot market).[64]

---

[64] The North American Electric Reliability Corporation (NERC) and the Federal Energy Regulatory Commission investigated both the 2014 polar vortex event and the 2011 freeze event that affected the Southwest and the Midwest. The findings for the 2014 study indicated that many recommendations for winter preparation made in the 2011 study had been implemented by the time of the polar vortex event. These actions along with emergency communications, the use of interruptible load, demand-side management tools, and voltage reduction significantly limited the need for involuntary load shedding in 2014. Nevertheless, NERC raised particular concerns about possible natural gas curtailment during a future freeze event, and recommended review and action by gas suppliers, regulators, and market participants.

Hurricanes, which are becoming more frequent and more severe as ocean temperatures rise, can also reduce a baseload coal plant's contribution to resilience. For example, a Category 4 hurricane that hit Texas in 2017 resulted in two coal-fired units having to switch to natural gas. The reason: on-site coal piles were too soaked with rainwater.[65]

Even with respect to normal outage rates, however, coal's advantage over more flexible natural gas is less than compelling. The North American Electric Reliability Corporation tracks outage rates by type of units using a five-year rolling average. Its 2016 expected forced outage rating for combined cycle natural gas units—which in most cases are the workhorses of the natural gas fleet—is in fact lower than that of coal plants.[66]

Therefore, considering the various *force majeure* climate events that have tested grid resilience in the past decade—hurricanes, extreme freezing, drought, and more frequent wildfires—it is increasingly apparent that resilience comes not from one type of generation resource. Rather, resilience on the grid of the future will depend on having a diversity of resources with a diversity of attributes. Baseload plants provide no singular panacea for resilience.

---

[65] One month after Hurricane Harvey hit the Texas Gulf Coast area, NRG Energy advised the Texas Public Utilities Commission (PUC) that it had switched its W.A. Parish units 5 and 6 from coal to natural gas because "the external coal pile at W.A. Parish became so saturated with rain water that the coal was unable to be delivered into the silos from the conveyer system." The two units, located just southwest of Houston, had a combined nameplate capacity of 1,468 megawatts. NRG Energy, letter filed in PUC Project No. 47552 on September 26, 2017. A week after Hurricane Harvey hit Texas, the threat from Hurricane Irma prompted Florida Power & Light to prepare for shutting down its Turkey Creek and St. Lucie nuclear plants, although only one unit had been shut down before the storm began to weaken.

[66] NERC's 2016 expected forced outage rate for combined cycle plants was 5.5%, compared to 8.8% for coal. While the size of a coal unit affected forced outage rates, even the best group score—7% for units 1,000 megawatts in size or larger—was higher than the rate experienced for combined cycle plants.

The use of slow-moving baseload gigaplants fit like a glove with the old monopoly paradigm of the regulatory contract. Locking up a huge amount of capital into a single asset was financially safe, because rate base guaranteed capital cost recovery from a captured customer base. Today, however, continued regulatory protection for gigaplants reduces the economic space in which competitive providers can operate. There is less justification for the protection because of how today's grid operates.

Therefore, if the concerns really are reliability and resilience, it makes little sense for a modern bulk power system to subsidize an aging multibillion dollar baseload plant. Investing in new flexible capacity would provide more resilience, and could cost the public much less.

While coal and nuclear gigaplants have provided special operational benefits in the past, there is no reason to assume they will be the only choices in the future, or even the best choices. The link between base load as a feature of the system's daily load profile and baseload generation was born of convenience and was never hard-wired. It worked well in the past, but the future will be different. The things that made baseload generators convenient are falling to a lower level of priority, and there are other cost-effective options for providing the same benefits.

Closing Thoughts

Many who are in the trenches of change know that the most challenging problems facing the modern electricity sector have no easy answers. One source of complexity is the interdisciplinary nature of the changes taking place. Engineers must learn how to think like lawyers; economists must think like biologists; and so on. The real story lies not in any single discipline's analysis, but in how the pieces fit together. That is the story I have tried to tell here.

I have taken pains throughout to explain my reasoning in detail, drawing on historical experience where useful. I do this from a desire for maximum transparency in explaining the reasoning behind my conclusions. For example, it would have been easy to simply offer my restatement of the public interest without explanation (making Chapter 2 considerably shorter). The "why" of it, however, is important. By laying bare the reasoning, I hope to challenge the reader to think more deeply about the changes, so that any point of disagreement can be traced to its true source for further consideration. Transparency is important in public policy dialogue, and it does not cease to be important when the subject is complex.

Reliance on well-tempered markets is a theme that runs throughout this book. No doubt many will find this difficult—some because they believe the pursuit of self-interest brings out the worst in people, others because they believe markets should not be tempered at all by concerns of the public interest or indeed regulation of any kind. Markets are imperfect, certainly; but it is hard to imagine better ways of promoting competition and choice if these two values are truly part of the new public interest. The use of imperfect markets is similar to Winston Churchill's maxim on how messy the democratic process can be: "No one pretends that democracy is perfect or all-wise. Indeed it has been said that democracy is the worst form of Government except for all those other forms that have been tried from time to time."[67]

The two issue areas briefly discussed in this afterword have both been contested vigorously in numerous cases, leaving them with plenty of grist for the mill of analysis. There are, however, other issues on the horizon that are just now taking form. Unlike net metering and the myth of baseload, they are not clashes between old world conventions and the future utility. Rather, they speak to the need to transition the new paradigm from one stage of socioeconomic evolution to the next. Defining and addressing

---

[67] Winston Churchill, House of Commons, 11 November 1947.

these new and more difficult problems will be virtually impossible without a careful conceptualization of what the future electric utility is.

For example, marginal cost pricing is a mainstay of sector reform to date. But increasingly regulators, stakeholders, and operators are questioning whether this powerful hammer inappropriately turns too many problems into nails. The concerns come laden with anecdotes, but anecdotes are not explanations. Baseload generator interests might claim that they don't make enough money through economic dispatch, therefore something must be wrong with the markets. Others might claim that greater penetration of subsidized renewables is distorting market prices (although segregating renewable energy subsidies from all other subsidies that have been at play as explained in Chapter 3 would itself distort the picture in a different way). Without letting go of all attachment to the status quo, solutions could drift towards a compounded mess of countervailing subsidies and inefficiencies that will end up costing the public more money.

Another closely related problem is how optimizing unit dispatch accounts for environmental impacts—or rather, how it doesn't. External mechanisms can augment energy revenues or offset costs: cap-and-trade emissions markets, renewable energy requirements, government subsidies for renewable energy, others. As with net metering, though, some of these external approaches are less than precise with respect to the dispatch choice and its environmental consequences. Even a carbon tax, which has been on a rollercoaster of interest for at least a decade, is essentially a clumsy add-on to marginal cost energy pricing. It is fine for bringing in new tax revenue, but lousy for providing dynamic price signals.[68]

One effect of these new and still-fuzzy lines of discontent has been calls to undo the evolution that has already taken place. Some have even called for a retreat from markets by subsidizing the largest (and dirtiest) plants on the system. Whether this has merit is its own lengthy discussion, but the fact that such a huge backward step has even been proposed at all is evidence that the sector may be entering into a new period of existential soul searching.

Finally, much in this book will no doubt seem like old news to many who have been in the thick of power sector analysis, planning, and regulation. To them, I would make this plea. We are approaching a time when what you know through experience and professional insight needs to be articulated to the wider public and in the context of a larger public interest. This involves much more than simply repeating to a lay audience the conclusions presented to your professional colleagues. What you see is important. How it connects with other parts of the socioeconomic environment is also important. However, the interdependence with other disciplines will often have its own calculus. What I have attempted to address in this book is how the pieces you see integrate with other pieces into a dynamic whole.

Defining the public interest is especially difficult, because doing so responsibly requires understand the bulk power system

---

[68] The poor price signals arise from the tax's rigid and administratively fixed rate. It can be shown easily that an administratively set value can result in no change to the dispatch outcome (and, therefore, to actual carbon emissions for a given operating period) while at the same time simply extracting more wealth from end-use customers. In contrast, a cap-and-trade system or a renewable portfolio standard involves an administratively determined quantitative outcome—a cap on the amount of emissions allowed or a minimum level of renewable energy usage—and allows market forces to determine the value based on the cost of reaching the quantitative targets. It is difficult to say which model will be the better fit in Utility of the Future version 2.0. My own hope is that we will find a new approach that is better than both.

along with the evolution of consumer preferences in an intimate, non-casual way. It is hard to do that from the outside. The sector is complicated and its interactions with non-sector actors are sometimes unclear. But its impact can be significant in many, many ways. That puts a burden on inside experts to understand the broad, interdependent picture, and to learn how to explain it. This is a formidable task of informed citizenry. It is not just about what can be done with new technology; it is about what ought to be done using the authority of the State.

Creative destruction is rapidly bringing the world of electricity to a critical and unavoidable juncture that requires a choice:

- deny the inevitable, prop up failing enterprises whose time has passed, and let future generations clean up the mess, or
- acknowledge and adapt to the change, and find ways now to make the transition easier for all who will be affected.

We can't do both.

Selected Bibliography

Aurobindo, Sri. *The Complete Works of Sri Aurobindo* (Pondicherry, India: Sri Aurobindo Ashram trust, 2003).

Buffett, Warren. Berkshire Hathaway's 2015 annual report.

Churchill, Winston. House of Commons, 11 November 1947.

Daly, Herman and Cobb, John. B. *For the Common Good: Redirecting the Economy toward Community, the Environment, and a Sustainable Future* (Boston: Beacon Street Press, 1994).

Einstein, Albert. "Einstein Reveals Text of Message," *New York Times*, August 29, 1948. (Published later under the title "Message to Intellectuals.")

Energy Information Administration. "Electric Power Annual." (1994-2017, including monthly updates).

Federal Energy Regulatory Commission and North American Electric Reliability Corporation. "Report on Outages and Curtailments During the Southwest Cold Weather Event of February 1-5, 2011" (August 2011).

Federal Power Commission. "Statistics of Electric Utilities in the United States." (1938-1979, including successor titles).

Federal Trade Commission. "Annual Report" (1935).

Hanh, Thich Nhat Hahn, *The Heart of the Buddha's Teaching* (Berkeley, CA: Parallax Press, 1998).

Jordan, Barbara. Statement on the Articles of Impeachment against President Richard M. Nixon, House Judiciary Committee, July 25, 1974.

King, Clyde, ed. *The Regulation of Municipal Utilities* (New York: D. Appleton and Co., 1912).

Mill, John Stuart. *Utilitarianism* (London: Parker, Son, and Bourn, 1863).

Munn v. State of Illinois, 94 U.S. 113; 24 L. Ed. 77 (1877).

North American Electric Reliability Corporation. "Polar Vortex Review" (September 2014).

Rawls, John. *Justice as Fairness: A Restatement* (Cambridge: Harvard University Press, 2001).

- - - - *A Theory of Justice* (Cambridge: Harvard University Press, 1971).

Schumpeter, Joseph A. *Capitalism, Socialism, and Democracy* (New York: Harper Perennial, 1942).

Texas Legislature, 76th regular session. Senate Bill 7, Relating to electric utility restructuring and to the powers and duties of the Public Utility Commission of Texas, Office of Public Utility Counsel, and Texas Natural Resource Conservation Commission; providing penalties (1999).

Index

clothed with a public interest, 5, 27-29, 183
public policy, 1, 5, 8, 15, 50, 55, 61-62, 118, 125, 131, 140, 146, 189, 192, 195-196, 207

rate base, 62, 71, 76, 80, 87, 190, 205
Rawls, John, 22
regional transmission organization (RTO), 9, 11, 81-83, 99, 108-110, 114-115, 117, 167-168, 175, 183-187
regulators, 2, 12-13, 37, 40, 48, 50, 52, 57-58, 65, 67, 79-80, 82, 88, 93, 100, 105-106, 115, 123-125, 130, 143-144, 159, 163, 168-175, 191, 195-196, 198, 207
regulatory contract, 5-7, 20-26, 34, 42-43, 45, 58, 63-64, 66-77, 80, 84-85, 87-89, 91-92, 95, 102, 105, 112, 120, 148, 156, 159-176, 190-191, 205
renewable, 14-15, 37, 47, 50, 63-64, 74, 81, 86, 89, 93, 114-115, 129-132, 144-146, 168, 172, 180-182, 185-186, 188, 191-192, 208
renewable portfolio standard (RPS), 131, 143, 145-146, 208
rent-seeking, 103-106, 117, 121, 163, 169
retail aggregation (buyers clubs), 14, 136-141, 190
retail customers, 5, 8, 11, 14-15, 74-76, 81, 86, 115, 120, 124, 129-130, 134-137, 142, 148, 157, 162 170, 184, 189, 192
retail price signals, 107, 114, 134-136
retail rates, 9, 107, 114, 136, 139, 148
retail service, 11, 36, 96, 98-100, 115, 117, 125, 128, 134, 137, 140, 142-144, 161, 170, 173-174, 180-185, 187-192
return on equity, 64, 66, 78
risk, *xii*, 6-7, 9, 15, 27, 40, 64, 70-73, 75, 78, 80-82, 84-85, 87, 89, 91-93, 97, 101-103, 110, 112, 115, 133-134, 154, 156, 165, 171, 176, 184, 187-188, 197

Schumpeter, Joseph, 7, 59-60, 62, 89-91, 195
Sherman Antitrust Act of 1890, 45
smart meters, 37, 86, 135-136, 138

About the Author

David J. Hurlbut is a senior analyst and economist at the National Renewable Energy Laboratory in Golden, Colorado. Prior to joining the lab in 2007 he was a senior economist at the Texas Public Utilities Commission, where he participated in the restructuring of the wholesale power market operated by the Electric Reliability Council of Texas and oversaw implementation of the state's successful renewable portfolio standard. He holds a doctorate and a master's degree from the Lyndon B. Johnson School of Public Affairs, University of Texas at Austin.